ROOTS WE GROW

ROOTS WE GROW

How Challenges, Opportunities, and Choices Shape the Lives We Build

Avi Shlanger

This book is intended for educational and inspirational purposes. The reflections and Growth prompts are designed to support personal growth, discussion, and learning.

First Edition

Published by
HOPE International Publishing
Israel

ISBN: 978-1-732-0186-2-4

For the next generation
and for those still growing along with them.

May your roots grow deep enough
to hold the life you are building
through the choices you make.

Grow deep.
Stand strong.

CONTENTS

INTRODUCTION

I used to think life moved in straight lines.
Work hard. Build security. Protect what you build.
Step by step. Year by year.

It didn't unfold that way. Not even close.
It bent.

It endured storms I did not plan for.

Trees don't grow in straight lines.
They grow toward light—around obstacles, through storms.

My life makes more sense as a tree than a timeline.

Roots I did not choose.
A trunk I built through discipline.
Storms that forced me to grow deeper.

This isn't a blueprint. It's a record.

Some seasons I handled well.
Some I'm still learning from.

If there is one thread that runs through these pages, it is this:
We build outward before we understand what's inside.

I am still rooted.
Still reaching.

You can be missing tools and still build.
You can be bruised and still become.

Roots grow in silence.
Storms don't build them. They reveal them.
This story grows the same way.

Each chapter returns to three things:

TREE WISDOM

Growth is rarely loud.
It happens underground first.

REFLECTION

A pause for perspective.
A moment to notice what just unfolded.

GROWTH

An invitation to notice your own seasons.

The rhythm stays the same:
Roots → Trunk → Branches → Seasons
Life moves forward, but it circles.

Sealing the Deal

The questions in the Growth section are not for reading alone. There is room to write your answers, even if writing doesn't come easily at first.

Writing may be challenging. It is for me too.

It can be slow, it can be tiring, and sometimes it feels like a chore you'd rather skip.

For a long time, I kept things in my head. They felt real in the moment, but they didn't stay. They shifted, and before I knew it, they were gone.

When a thought stays inside, it disappears the moment something else takes your attention. Putting it in ink—no matter how messy or crooked—gives it a place to land.

Ink turns a thought into something you can see.

Don't worry about the "straightness" of your lines. This writing is for you.

Once a thought is on the page, it's there. You can't move around it the same way.

Writing became a way for me to hold myself to something.

Growth isn't about how much you read. It's about the commitments you make to yourself.

A Note for the Reader

This isn't a blueprint. It's the path I followed when my main road was blocked. There were places I didn't fit, rooms that felt tight before I even sat down. I remember the empty notebook, and the label that came with it.

If you feel out of sync with the system you're in, you aren't broken. You may simply be uncalibrated for the room.

This is for the person tired of trying to fit into something that was never designed for them.

Stop trying to fix the wiring. Start building an environment that respects it.

TREE WISDOM

Growth begins where no one is watching.

REFLECTION

I started to understand my life more clearly when I took the time to reflect.

GROWTH

1. Your Season

If your life were a tree right now, what would it be working on—strengthening roots, thickening the trunk, extending branches, or protecting fruit?

CHAPTER 1

ROOTED AND REACHING

The First Rhythm

Jerusalem held its mild weather most of the year. The rain was a rare, hesitant visitor.

In our neighborhood, there wasn't a bus to take me to school. Even if there had been, we didn't have the fare.

So I walked.

The route was the same every morning and every afternoon, three miles each way. After a few months, I knew every crack in the pavement by heart. The same broken curb. The same loose stone that shifted under my foot every morning. That walk became the first rhythm of my life. My body learned it before my mind did.

Start.
Keep going.
You will arrive.

When you walk six miles a day as a kid, you don't just learn geography. You learn persistence, patience, and timing. And over time, you begin to understand that the distance doesn't change, but your capacity to handle it does. You figure out how to keep moving, even when the destination feels like a ghost on the horizon. I didn't call it discipline back then. I just called it "what you do."

The Table

For me, childhood didn't begin with dreams of the future. It began with watching how adults carried the weight of the present, day after day.

Our kitchen table was not a place for long, wandering conversations. It was a cold surface where decisions were made quietly, where bills were paid with tired hands and heavy thoughts.

As a boy, I understood a fundamental truth without a single word of explanation:
Life wasn't going to hand out much.
If we wanted to build something, we were going to have to source the raw materials ourselves.

That was the rhythm at home. And outside, it didn't feel much different.

The Boot with the Hole

I was seven years old, walking to school at 7:00 a.m. One morning, the rain came down with a vengeance. Jerusalem winters have a sharp, high-altitude wind that cuts through fabric like a blade.

The only boots I had were hand-me-downs, and there was a jagged hole in the left one. Still, I wore them.

By the time I reached the school gates, my left sock was soaked. It wasn't just damp. It was heavy. It was the kind of wet that pulls your attention back to your toes when you're supposed to be listening to the teacher.

At school, I'd peel the sock off and hide it behind the radiator to dry. The heat barely reached it, but I checked anyway. It usually took two hours of shivering before I felt whole again. Then I'd put it back on and do it all over again. It was just a boot with a hole. At the time, it felt bigger than that.

Only later did I understand what that moment meant:
Innovation often begins with a lack of resources.

On the way home, I stopped by the local bicycle shop. I didn't ask for a handout. Instead, I asked how much it would cost for the plastic and glue so I could fix it myself. The owner looked at the boot, then at me.

"This fix is on me," he said. I didn't say much. I just nodded and held onto the moment.

There was no speech, no pity, and no questions. That was the backbone of the neighborhood.

People helped when they could, and they didn't turn it into a performance. They knew the struggle, and they respected the kid who was trying to solve it.

The Mismatch: A Body and Brain Out of Sync

School felt like a game where the rules were written in a language I couldn't speak, and I was playing with the wrong hand. Sitting in a room for eight hours not understanding a word isn't learning; it's a slow-motion sentence.

I'm a lefty in a system built for the right.

Because Hebrew moves from right to left, my hand didn't smear the words as I wrote them.

But that didn't stop the friction. The teachers were obsessed with a specific kind of "structure."

They wanted the pen held at a precise angle and my body squared to the desk.

It didn't feel like a classroom; it felt like a cage for my left arm.

The teachers didn't just want me to learn.

They wanted me to conform.

To the teachers, my natural way of moving was a "disorder" that needed to be corrected. They prioritized the appearance of the notebook over my struggle. They saw the way I contorted my body to see the page and called it "clumsy." They saw my irregular grip and called it "unstructured."

When a system prioritizes the “look” of the work over the "logic" of the worker, the unique thinkers are always the first to be discarded.

I was trying to navigate a world that was physically and mentally built for someone else. In that classroom, being "different" was treated as a failure of discipline rather than a variation of design.

The real issue was simple and impossible to hide:
I couldn’t write what people could read, and I couldn’t read what others wrote.

I remember the room more than the lessons. I remember the screech of chalk on the board, the white dust on the teacher’s fingertips, and the synchronized scratching of thirty pencils moving in a rhythm I couldn't join. I stared at the paragraph on the board like it was a sheer stone wall.

I wanted to climb it.
I couldn't find a single foothold.

I’d copy one word, erase it, and try again. I pressed so hard the lead would snap. My notebook looked like a battlefield. I tried to make it look like progress, even when it wasn’t.

There was no diagnosis. No one said "dyslexia." There was only the daily, stinging fact that my head and my left hand were in a constant state of civil war.

When people don't understand the struggle inside you, they usually decide you're just being difficult.

The Shield of the Troublemaker

When you can't succeed through the front door, you start looking for another way in. Over time, I became the class clown, the troublemaker, the boy who made noises just to get sent out. Laughs were a shield. It was easier to control the noise than sit in the silence. If they were laughing *with* me, they weren't looking at my empty notebook.

But soccer gave me what the classroom took away: Confidence.
On the field, literacy didn't matter. Timing, movement, and teamwork were the only languages spoken. If you were on my team, we usually won. People wanted to be on my team. In that world, I wasn't "broken." I was a high-value asset. The teachers, however, didn't see the athlete. They saw the "problem." I remember a teacher grabbing me by the ear, twisting hard, and physically throwing me out of the room. The pain was secondary to the look in his eyes: the look that says you're not worth the time it takes to teach you.

I was trying not to be humiliated every day. When you can't succeed the normal way, you find another way to feel in control, even if it's the wrong way.

The Shelter Years

When I was nine, the Six-Day War reached our building. We lived near the border, close enough that the war didn't feel like news; it felt like a physical vibration in the floorboards. The sirens cut through the day like sharpened metal, and suddenly, the rhythm of school and soccer vanished.

People moved quickly, but not in a blind panic. It was more like they already knew the choreography of survival. We gathered in the underground shelter along with the other tenants from our building and the surrounding blocks. The air was damp and heavy, smelling of cold concrete, old blankets, and the stale cigarette smoke trapped in a room that wasn't allowed to breathe.

Someone had a small radio. The volume stayed low, a tinny hum against the silence, but everyone leaned toward it like it was a campfire. Every few minutes, the broadcast would be drowned out by distant cracks—machine-gun bursts—and then heavier explosions that made white dust drift down from the ceiling like ghost-rain.

Babies cried, stopped, and then cried again. The adults spoke in half-sentences, their voices hushed as if the bombers above could hear them. We slept on the floor for six days, packed together close enough to feel everyone else's fear, even if no one had the words to express it.

Time didn't move the same down there. It stretched.

Through it all, my father sat steady. As a Holocaust survivor, he didn't panic. He sat there like a man who had already learned a lesson the rest of us were still figuring out:
You can't control the storm.
You can only control how you sit inside it.

Neighbors brought food and water, sharing it quietly, treating survival as a communal task rather than a private struggle.

I didn't have the vocabulary for it then, but you learn something in a place like that. Even when you are terrified, you keep breathing. You wait. You get through the hour in front of you, and you realize that the walls may shake, but you are still standing.

The Small Promise

Growing up under that kind of pressure teaches you to make small promises. You don't make the big promises like in the movies. You make the small ones you can actually keep.

Mine was simple: Try again tomorrow.

I didn't need a teacher's permission to say it. I didn't need a bank account or a clean notebook to say it. I could say it even on a day when everything went wrong, when the school skipped me by, or when the sirens sent us back underground.

That promise stayed with me, tucked away where no one could see it. It didn't make any noise and it didn't show up on my report card, but it became the foundation of my roots. It was quiet, invisible, and unbreakable.

By eleven, I understood two things:

1. The world was not going to slow down and wait for me to figure out its written rules.

2. I could still be useful if I showed up where hands, heart, and timing mattered.

That was the moment work entered the picture. And once work entered, the entire landscape shifted. It wasn't because life got easier, but because I finally found a place where the way my brain worked was an advantage, not a disability.

TREE WISDOM

Roots grow in the soil they are given.

These were root years.
The kind where strength builds underneath.

REFLECTION

I didn't get confidence from school.
I got it from doing—walking, figuring things out, learning as I went.

And I kept promises to myself:
Try again tomorrow.
Start.
    Keep going.
        You will arrive.

Some things don't look like much from the outside.
But they carry more than you think.

GROWTH

1.The Validation Gap

If the "official system" (school or corporate HR) didn't exist, what is one skill you have that would still make you valuable?

2.The Invisible Shield

Think of the last time you felt embarrassed or "less than." Did you use a joke or anger to hide it?
What would happen if you just sat steady in that "storm" instead?

3.The Quiet Fix

The bicycle shop owner helped without a speech.
Who in your life is currently "walking with a hole in their boot," and what small, quiet fix can you offer them today?

CHAPTER 2

THIN SOIL, STRONG ROOTS (1970-1973)

Early Market Mornings and Late-Night Bread Trucks

There is a moment in every young life when childhood quietly steps aside, almost without notice.
No ceremony. No announcement.

Just a growing understanding that the people around you are carrying more than you realized, and that you will soon have to carry something too. That moment came for me earlier than I expected, and it didn't ask permission. I started working when I was eleven.

Most mornings I woke up at 6:00 a.m. and walked to school like I belonged there. I stayed long enough for roll call, then I left my things and disappeared into a different kind of day. It didn't feel like escape. It felt necessary. My friends covered for me—moving my bag from classroom to classroom and telling teachers I was in the bathroom or somewhere else.

They weren't trying to turn me into a rebel. They were trying to protect me the only way they knew how.

[Quick note for teenagers reading:
I found my way around it back then. It worked for a while, but it wasn't the best way through it.
If school feels challenging for you, the answer isn't to disappear.
It's to find the right support—and the right way to learn for you.]

The Currency of the Classroom

Back then, school felt like a daily setup.
In the classroom, literacy was the only currency, and I was already bankrupt before the first bell rang.

Work was different. It made sense in a way school never did.

It was a place where effort counted,
where hands mattered, and where you could earn respect without needing a clean page.

Market Physics

By around 10:00 a.m., I would arrive at the vegetable market.

The market was loud and alive in a way that woke you up, even when you were already tired from the day. Trucks backed into narrow spaces. Men shouted directions. Tailgates dropped with a heavy thud. Cart wheels squeaked; scales clicked.

Coins changed hands fast, as if money itself had somewhere to be.

I remember the first time I walked into the market looking for work. I tried to look like I knew what I was doing.
I didn't, but I hoped no one would notice.

A driver stood on the tailgate with a cigarette tucked in the corner of his mouth. He didn't ask my name. He nodded at a stack of crates and said, "You want to work, start there."

His voice wasn't harsh. It was just busy.

I slid my hands under the first crate and felt the truth right away. It was heavier than it looked, the kind of weight that surprises your hands before your body catches up. My fingers went numb from the pressure, and my shoulder did a quick calculation: lift wrong, and you'll pay for it later.

I shifted my grip, anchored my weight, and stood.

The crate didn't just have mass; it had a lesson. It scraped my shirt on the way up. I remember thinking, don't drop it. Don't be the kid who drops it.

I carried it to the stall and set it down as gently as I could, like the fruit had a bruise limit.
The stall owner didn't say anything. He just kept moving.
But he didn't correct me either.

That was my first tiny win.
Not praise, but permission to keep going.

The Currency of Effort

Hours later, when the shift ended, someone pressed coins into my palm. It wasn't a lot, but the weight of them felt louder than anything I'd experienced in school.

My hands were sore. My shirt smelled like citrus.
And for once, my effort was something I could actually hold, not something someone else had to measure for me.

The job was simple: loading and unloading crates from the truck bed to the stalls. Some crates were fifty pounds, sometimes more than my own weight. I learned quickly which ones you hope for—lettuce—and which ones you didn't—potatoes and watermelons.

The market had rules, but they weren't written anywhere—you learned them by getting it wrong.

Don't bruise the produce.
Keep the flow moving.

If you lifted wrong, your body paid for it.
If you stacked wrong, you paid for it with a crash.

If you slowed at the wrong moment, someone yelled your name like it was your full legal identity. So I learned the only way you really learn in a place like that: I watched, I listened, and I copied what worked.

I tested the weight of a crate quickly and if it shifted, I adjusted before committing. Drivers liked someone who moved with confidence; stall owners liked stacks that didn't lean.

I tried to become both.

The Currency of Choice

I was the one who showed up on weekdays while everyone else was in school. I took whatever work was available, usually about three times a week. The money wasn't extra to me.

It mattered. It gave me something I needed at the time: Choices.

I could choose to ride the bus and walk less, or I could buy a falafel and walk the entire way home on a full belly. Most days, I chose the falafel. I loved falafel.

I was learning, slowly but clearly, that my time had a market value.

The work paid about seven dollars for four hours. By today's standards, that would be worth about twenty-five. The market had its own order. Prices changed with the heat, the supply, and the season, but the rhythm stayed steady.

In that world, I didn't need clean handwriting.
I needed attention and timing.

People noticed when they didn't have to repeat themselves. A nod from a driver or a stall owner meant more to me than a grade I couldn't earn.

After the shift, I'd go back to school and pick up my things. Most teachers didn't mind my absence. I wasn't causing trouble in their classrooms, and it meant there was one less student for them to manage.

They were happy for the silence.
I was happy for the work.

The Street Was Another Classroom

The walk home was through blocks that didn't care about your age or your story. These neighborhoods were a mix of languages and faces: families from a dozen different countries trying to build lives in a country that was still learning how to be itself.

The blocks were rough and crowded. Older boys watched the corners like they owned the pavement. When I started earning money from the vegetable market, they noticed.

In that world, money has a scent.

One afternoon, I was walking home with my earnings. I could feel the coins in my pocket; they had a weight that made me feel capable. But that weight also made me a target.

I turned a corner and saw them before they noticed me. Three boys. Older. Sitting on a low wall. I had a choice: turn around and show fear or walk straight through the friction.

I didn't turn around. I kept my pace steady. I knew that in the market, if you hesitate with a heavy crate, you drop it. The street was no different. You don't negotiate with a threat; you navigate it.

They stood up as I got closer. Their leader was a head taller than me; his eyes already locked on my pockets.

"You've been busy, haven't you?" he said. It wasn't a question.
My stomach tightened. It wasn't dramatic; it was instant. It was as if my body knew what was happening before the brain could even finish the sentence. One of them looked up and nodded toward me, acting as if we were friends—as if this was normal.

"Come here."

In that moment, you don't get a speech.
You get choices.

You run and risk being chased, or you stand and risk the fight. At first, I was afraid. You feel it before you think it. That fear taught me two things fast: when to run and when to defend myself with my fists.

Sometimes I got beat up and lost the money.
Sometimes I ran.
I ran hard, not stopping until my lungs burned and I could taste metal in my mouth, pushing past the point where stopping felt easier.

As I grew stronger, they left me alone. Some of them even became friends. They tried to pull me into bullying others, but I wasn't cut out for that. Respect mattered to me; cruelty did not.

That sentence is still true today.

In business, in family, in friendships, in leadership—in life—respect lasts. Cruelty always comes back with a bill.

Night Belonged to Bread

To keep busy and make more money, my night shifts belonged to the bread factory.

I would arrive around 7:00 p.m., after a forty-minute walk to get there.

I always wished I had a bike. Sometimes a neighbor would let me borrow his, and I could get there in fifteen minutes.

The factory was a different world than the vegetable market, but it followed its own kind of logic. The market was about the sun and the soil; the factory was about the heat and the machine.

The air was thick with the scent of yeast and the sound of industrial rhythm.

In the factory, I found a logic that worked for my brain. The machines didn't care about my handwriting or my dyslexia. They only cared about my timing. If I stayed in sync with the line, the system worked. If I faltered, the entire operation felt the friction. My job was simple: loading the bread onto trucks for early morning deliveries.
But in a high-speed operation, “simple” doesn’t mean “easy.”

While the city began to quiet down, I moved between the warm racks and the empty truck beds. The drivers wouldn't arrive for hours, but the work couldn't wait. In that industrial space, I was the one responsible for the final stage of the loading process.

I wasn't being watched. I was being trusted—and that changed how I showed up.
In a bread factory, time is the only currency that matters. I didn't have a supervisor breathing down my neck; I just had a deadline and a destination. I developed a system for the load, calculating the height, the balance, and the weight of the trays so they wouldn't shift during the sharp turns of the Jerusalem hills.

I wanted the trucks to be perfect before the first engine turned over.

There was a specific kind of satisfaction in that work, the kind that stayed with you after you left. I moved with a rhythm that school never allowed:
Lift.
Slide.
Stack.

I wasn't fighting a textbook; I was managing a workflow. We all wanted the same thing: to finish the job, close the tailgates, and go home.

In business, efficiency isn't just about speed.
It is about closing the loop so the next shift can start without friction.

By the time I slammed the last heavy door shut, the factory felt different. The chaos of the ovens was over. The trucks were staged and ready. I finished around 11:00 p.m., leaving behind a finished product that didn't need a single word of explanation.
The work spoke for itself.

Tight, Not Fast

One night, I learned a lesson the hard way. I was in a rush to finish early, thinking I could save a few minutes by cutting corners. I rolled a rack in and started stacking, but in my haste, I left a small space between two crates. It was a tiny gap, barely enough to notice unless you were specifically looking for it.

An older worker, a man who had spent decades in the heat of that room, walked past and stopped without a word. He didn't yell or lecture me. He simply put his hand on the side of my stack and pushed, gently.

The column shifted.

It wasn't a collapse; it was a warning. He pointed at the dark gap between the plastic edges and spoke with the authority of someone who had seen thousands of loads fail on the road.

"That space becomes a slide," he said.

Then he began to move. He tightened the crates, corner to corner, until the whole stack felt like one solid piece of stone. No drama. No anger. Just precision.

"Tight," he said. "Not fast."
After that, my arms still worked hard, but my brain worked even harder.

I realized that speed without stability is just a faster way to fail.

In the warehouse, and later in business, I learned that a "small gap" in the foundation always creates a disaster at the destination.
I stopped chasing speed.
I started chasing stability.

Respect Collects Interest

Being reliable brought small advantages. A driver would save me the last bottle of cold water. A stall owner would call my name first when he needed help, letting me take the extra hour of work.

It was the small things that kept me going.

Time and sweat were my first currency; respect was the interest that collected over time.

Of course, there were hard parts. Tiredness arrived early and tried to stay for the duration of the shift. Some nights I felt the weight in my forearms even after I put the last crate down.

I learned to keep my back straight and let my legs carry what they were built to carry. I learned to drink water before I was thirsty and to eat when I could, not just when I felt like it.

The market demanded a steady rhythm, and I gave it exactly what it asked for.

Money was small. Meaning was not.

At the market, I moved what grew from the ground. At night, I loaded what we made from it.
The loop felt honest. I didn't have words for it back then, but the idea took shape while I stacked bread and counted crates in my head.

Roots were already in place from the walks and the quiet promises, but the trunk comes from steady days that hold weight—from repeating a small job until it becomes part of how you move through life. The market and the bread factory gave me that.

None of it came to punish me for what I couldn't do at school.

It came for me, to teach me pace, order, and the value of keeping the middle clear so everything else can pass through.

My report card was not worth the time to read.
To this day, I don't know how I even passed.

But I knew how to show up—and people counted on me.

That was enough for a beginning.

TREE WISDOM

A tree grows stronger by doing the same thing over and over—not in the big, loud moments, but in the steady, silent ones.

REFLECTION

Work was simple. Show up. Match the pace. Keep the flow steady.

The phrase "Tight, not fast" didn't stay behind at the bread factory. It followed me into everything I did. In a factory, when things are loose, they eventually fall. You end up wasting time going back to fix what should have been done right the first time.

Efficiency is not having to go back.

Whether you are loading a truck or leading a team, the same rules apply. If the foundation is shaky, speed doesn't help. At some point, you will have to stop and deal with what didn't hold.
What stayed with me:

- Test the weight before you commit your full strength.
- Keep things tight, not just fast.
- Pay attention to where you stand, especially when others are depending on the ground you hold.

GROWTH

1.Starting Before Ready

Where in your life are you waiting to feel ready instead of starting with what you already have?

What would change if you treated your energy the way you treat your money?

2.The Handoff

Think of a project or a relationship where you are the bridge.

How can you make your part of the handoff cleaner so the next person doesn't have to fix what you left loose?

3.Earning Self-Trust

What is something small you can do daily that would build trust in yourself?

CHAPTER 3

HARD GROUND, HARD LESSONS (1973-1977)

The Real Sea

By fourteen, I wanted the sea. Not the romantic versions from movies, but the real one. I wanted the kind of sea that doesn't care who you are. The kind that humbles you and teaches you balance in your bones.

I wanted to travel the world. More than that, I wanted a future that wasn't a classroom with a teacher staring at my notebook like it proved I didn't belong.

I wasn't escaping responsibility.
I was trying to find the right kind.

So instead of going into high school the normal way, I took a different route. I tested and interviewed for the Navy Boarding Academy.

When I got accepted, it didn't feel like "success."
It felt like oxygen, like someone finally opened a door and said, "Okay. Try it your way."

The Academy was a system with rules, but they were physical rules. It was a structure I could finally understand because it was built on action, not just theory.

For the first time, I wasn't fighting the room.
I was learning how to navigate the world.

The First Day I Put on a Uniform

The academy gave me structure that held me. They gave me a uniform, a metal locker, and a bed that was mine. They fed me three hot meals a day.

Those things sound small. They weren't.

A uniform meant I was a part of something larger than myself.
A locker meant my life finally had a place.
Scheduled meals meant I wouldn't be forgotten that day.

The first time I put on the uniform, the fabric felt stiff against my skin, like it had rules of its own. I looked at myself and had a strange thought: This is what it looks like when someone expects you to show up.

My shoulders sat differently. My chin lifted without asking permission.

It wasn't pride.
It was relief.

It was as if I didn't have to invent myself every morning from scratch. I didn't have to find a way to belong.
The uniform did it for me.

Dorm life was basic: four beds, one narrow aisle, and no privacy. We shared showers and bathrooms, but it didn't feel like punishment. It felt like order.

Most of the boys there came from some kind of broken or complicated home. We were immigrant families, poor families, and families carrying pain they didn't know how to talk about. It made the room feel equal. Nobody needed to pretend.

For the first time, I wasn't the "problem kid."
I was just one of the boys.

The Name That Fit

From day one, I stopped answering to my given name, Kalman. I started introducing myself as Avi.

The first time someone said "Avi" back to me, my body answered before my mind did. My shoulders loosened. My stomach unclenched. It felt simple, like the name didn't snag on anything.

"Kalman" carried echoes I didn't want.
"Avi" was just me. Clean. No apology.

It wasn't a dramatic reinvention. It was a name that didn't invite jokes. A name that didn't come with a story I didn't want to explain.

Some people change a name because it sounds cool.
I changed mine because I wanted a fresh start so badly, I could taste it.

A name doesn't fix your life.
But it can change how you walk into it.

A Different Kind of Intelligence

The academy ran on a steady clock. Early mornings. Inspections. Drills. Meals on time. Lights out. That rhythm did something important for me: it quieted the chaos.

When your childhood is unstable, your nervous system is always scanning. You are constantly listening for silence, footsteps, tone changes, or doors slamming. In an unpredictable home, those are the early warning signs of trouble.

Structure quieted the noise.

Because the system was predictable, I didn't have to scan the room all the time. It gave my brain less to fear and more space to focus.

I still struggled with homework and tests; that didn't disappear.
But something fundamental changed:
I stopped thinking of my struggle as an obstacle.

Instead, I started treating my dyslexia like a challenge with a solution.

I knew I needed support.
So I made deals.

I had physical strength and I had courage, and I used both.
When I saw bullying, I stepped in.

I didn't do it for attention or applause. I did it because I never respected cruelty.

I made a professional trade.

In exchange for protection, some of the boys helped me study. They explained the concepts I couldn't understand alone. They helped me prepare for tests that otherwise would have buried me.

We built an unofficial system:

I protected the weak.
They helped me learn.
We all survived better.

That was my first real lesson in partnership.

Today, people call it networking, teamwork, or collaboration.
In truth, it's older than business.
It's human.

I learned that you don't have to be perfect at everything to be valuable. You need to understand your weaknesses and know how to embrace them and then trade your strengths for what you lack.

My weaknesses didn't end me.
They pushed me toward people.

Sharm el-Sheikh and the Sea That Doesn't Negotiate

My dream had come true.

At age 18, when my service began, I was stationed in Sharm el-Sheikh. The Red Sea is beautiful, but beauty can still be strict. The deck moves even when the water looks calm. The horizon is steady, but your body isn't.

For two weeks at a time, the ship was my home.

My stomach did not agree with the sea. Not even a little. I spent the first weeks in a state of constant, physical rebellion. I tried to ignore it. I tried to "tough it out." But the sea doesn't care about your willpower.

You don't negotiate with the sea. You adapt to it.

I started carrying a bucket around with me. It wasn't dignified and it certainly wasn't the heroic image I had in my head, but it was effective. That bucket taught me another fundamental lesson in Operational Reality:
Stop arguing with the facts.
Solve the actual problem.

I used to think that pushing through a physical limitation was the only definition of strength. It wasn't. Being practical worked better. Sometimes the strongest thing you can do is admit, "This isn't for me," and then build a system that allows you to keep going anyway.

Acceptance is not surrender.
It is the first step toward a solution.

I've seen the same thing later in business, pushing through something that clearly isn't working, instead of adjusting early. We ignore the "sea sickness" of our projects until they capsize. The bucket taught me that once you stop pretending the problem doesn't exist, you can finally get back to work.

One Week Off

After two weeks at sea, we received one week off. Most of the guys went home to rest. I didn't really have a home that felt like rest, and I loved the beach, so I stayed on the naval base.

There's a particular kind of quiet on a base when the crowd leaves. There is less noise, less performance, and more space. The air feels wider. You can hear the wind and your own thoughts.

For a nervous system that is always scanning for trouble, silence is the ultimate luxury.

One afternoon, while swimming, I caught a glimpse of a girl sunbathing on the beach. We talked easily. No pressure. No games. I joked and asked her if she could teach me how to swim. She laughed. I invited her to see my boat that evening. She came.

We spent the next couple of days of her vacation, and mine, getting to know each other. It was enough to stay in contact after she returned home.

For the first time in a long time, my life didn't feel like a fight. It felt like a beginning.

The Call into the Office

In the summer of 1975, our ship arrived at the shipyard after a border patrol. We were cleaning the deck, lost in the regular routine of salt and steel, when the captain called me into his office.

The office felt too quiet after the deck. The door closed with a soft click that sounded final. There was a fan somewhere, steady and indifferent, and the light in the room was flatter than outside. No sky. No wind. No escape.

My hands didn't know what to do.
So I kept them still.

I stared at a spot on his desk like it could tell me what was coming. When he said the words, my throat tightened like I'd swallowed something dry. My stomach dropped, not like fear, like the floor moved an inch beneath my boots.

I remember thinking one senseless, practical thought:
How do I get home fast?

That's what shock does.
It doesn't give you poetry; it gives you logistics.

That walk from the deck to the office is still etched into my body. You don't know why you're being called. Your mind runs through a thousand possibilities, searching for a reason that makes sense.

Did I do something wrong?
Did someone accuse me?
Am I in trouble?

The captain's face told me it wasn't about discipline. He didn't use his "captain" voice. He looked at me with the eyes of a man who was about to break a world.

He told me my father had died.

Family Matters

In Israel, burial happens fast. There wasn't time to process; only time to move.

On the flight home, I didn't cry. At this stage in my life, I'd forgotten how. In the world I grew up in, men didn't cry. You didn't show weakness.

You swallowed it and kept walking.

I felt worry first: about my family and about what I would find when I arrived. I tried to hold my thoughts like a container without a lid. When the plane landed at Ben Gurion, I hitchhiked home with a blank stare on my face, saying nothing but my address.

Three weeks before, my mother told me my father wasn't doing well. He had lost the maintenance job he had held for over twenty years. At age fifty, his pride was bruised and his spirit was tired.

She didn't say it dramatically.
She said it the way people speak when they've been carrying something alone, and their arms finally give out, "There's been a crisis at home, but it will get better".

But this crisis was the kind where everyone starts walking quieter afterward. This was not the first sign that life had become heavy for my dad.

Soon after, he found a job as a security guard. It should have been a lifeline. A paycheck. A reason to get up in the morning and keep moving.

But the job came with a weapon.
And when a person is already sinking, access to something like that can turn one dark moment into a final decision.

On the first day of work, after receiving his uniform and a gun, he took his own life. That is how my father died.

Beyond Walls

We went to the cemetery with a quiet that wasn't peaceful. It was controlled. It was the kind of quiet where you feel that if anyone opens their mouth the wrong way, something inside the family will split.

I didn't know all the rules yet, but I could feel them.

We didn't walk the path that everyone else walks to bury their loved ones. We walked past the main rows, past the places where names sit together like they belong. We kept going. It wasn't far, but far enough to feel it in my body.

We buried him outside the walls.

A side place.
A separation you don't need explained.

Even as a teenager, I felt what it meant. It wasn't only about where the body goes; it was about where the family gets placed.

In the center, you belong.
Outside the walls, you're marked.

In those days, in many communities, suicide didn't only break a family; it labeled it.

People didn't ask questions. They assumed. Some whispered. Some looked away. Sometimes even the burial carried that judgment, like grief wasn't enough on its own.

Nobody had to say it out loud. In families like ours, shame didn't come as a speech.

It came as directions.
It came as where you're allowed to stand.

I remember staring at the ground and thinking one senseless, practical thought:
So even in death, he can't rest with the others.

That thought hit me harder than the funeral.

Grief is heavy, but judgment is sharp.
Grief says, "we lost someone."
Judgment says, "And we'll make sure you feel it."

My mother and sister stood tight-faced, like they had pulled every emotion back behind their eyes and locked the door. We all stood:

Still.
Hard.
Quiet.

Some of the adults around us that day were Holocaust survivors. They had learned to bury pain so deep it turned into stone. They taught their children the same rule without ever saying it out loud:

Feel it later, if you must. First, survive.

We came back from the cemetery to the apartment. The silence followed us through the door.

The Empty Shiva

And now came the part that was supposed to hold you.

In Israel, people come to your house and sit with you after the burial. It's called Shiva, the front door stays open, neighbors bring food, and friends sit close so the silence doesn't swallow you whole.

But very few came.

No voices in the hallway.
No trays in the kitchen.
No comforting circle of people filling the room with ordinary life.

It was just us.

The apartment was small on a normal day, already stuffy. That week it became unbearable, like the air itself was crowded. Like every breath had to squeeze past the silence first.

I did what I knew how to do.
I showed up.
I helped.
I handled the practical pieces because emotions had nowhere to land.

I became useful. Not because I was strong, but because I didn't know any other option.

Under all of it—the corner of the cemetery, the empty apartment, the week that should have been full of people—one sentence formed in me. It wasn't poetic. It wasn't spiritual.
It was just survival math: If I stop moving, I will break.
So I kept moving.

Later, much later, I would understand what discipline can become in a family like mine.
It isn't a virtue. It's a life raft.
It doesn't calm the storm. It just keeps you from drowning in it.

Self-discipline doesn't erase loss.
It just gives you a way to keep moving while you carry it—until you choose to lay it down.
That week didn't teach me how to grieve.
It taught me how to function.

The Vault of Silence

I didn't make any grand promise to myself.
I made a small one, the kind you can keep even when your chest feels split:

Start.
    Keep going.
        You will arrive.

In our family, tears weren't a language. Work was. Once a person learns that, he starts building his life like a bridge. It isn't designed to look pretty; it is designed to hold weight.

But even bridges have limits.

In the short moments we spoke as a family, we tried to piece together what happened.

My father had been fired from his job as a maintenance man at an Israeli weapons company. After surviving the Holocaust, we guessed he felt stripped of his dignity. He couldn't handle life anymore.

And the damage didn't stop there.

My older sister couldn't contain the pressure either. She started hanging with the wrong crowd and took substances to dilute the emotional pain. Little did we all know, at the age of twenty-two, she would be admitted to a mental hospital for mental illness she never came back from.

This, too, was added to the growing vault of blame and shame.

I locked it up inside me and lived as if the vault didn't exist. With time, I tried to forget that it was even there.

The Pivot

The army officers stepped in. They wanted me closer to home to help my family; they were probably worried for my sanity because of the weight surrounding it: the suicide, the mental illness, and the silence.

I was sent back to the recruitment station to find a new position closer to home. The offer sounded almost too perfect: Firefighter in the Air Force.
Two weeks on duty, two weeks at home.

It was a relief. No more carrying buckets at sea. I could be closer to home, and more importantly, closer to my girlfriend.

I used my free time like a life float.

Two or three evenings a week, I'd hitchhike to Bat Yam to see her. I slept on the floor beside her bed because there wasn't another room in her family's small apartment.

To me, it felt like home.
There was nothing left for me at my own house.

Home wasn't a place anymore.
It was where I could breathe.

The Crooked Finger

I finished the course, and the captain liked me. He wanted me to become an instructor for firefighters, and that became my post for the remainder of my three-year service.

For fun, I played on a soccer team with my army friends. One late afternoon, I was running toward the goal when someone hit me from behind. I flew into the air and catapulted into the goal post.

My right-hand pinky was severed.

My friends searched for the detached finger, found it, and rushed me to the hospital. It was reconnected, but even today, it doesn't fully work. It stays crooked. It will never be straight.

I'm grateful it was on my right hand.

As an instructor, it didn't affect my work. And honestly, I didn't give it much weight then, and I don't now. People ask about it, but in my memory, it leaves no mark.

It is what it is.
A casualty of living and having fun.

What stayed with me wasn't the injury.
It was what my friends did, they cared.
They searched for the missing part. They helped me. They didn't leave me alone in it.

It was one finger.
It healed, crooked.
Life moved on.

Some scars are just physical.
The ones that matter are the ones you can't see.

Folding the Uniform

By 1977, the rhythm of orders and inspections came to an end. I was twenty-one years old, and I was folding my uniform for the last time. It didn't feel like leaving a job. It felt like shedding a skin.

I finally felt free. It wasn't the light, airy freedom of a vacation. It was the heavy, solid freedom of a man who finally owns his own time.
I was finally my own person.

For years, my life had been defined by the structures of others. First, the school system that didn't want me. Then, the market that needed my labor. Finally, the military that required my obedience.

I was done with roll calls.
I was done with commanders.
I was done with anyone telling me who I was allowed to be.

In the military, the uniform does the talking for you. It tells people your rank, your history, and your worth before you even open your mouth. But as I placed that fabric into the locker for the last time, I realized the silence was up to me now.

Agency is the ultimate professional asset.
When you are no longer a component in a machine, you have to become the engineer of your own life. The "structure" was gone. The "cage" was open. I was twenty-one and I was exactly where I wanted to be:
At the beginning.

TREE WISDOM

Storms don't break a tree just because they arrive.
They reveal where the wood is brittle and where the roots have held.
A storm doesn't create strength; it tests what was already built in the quiet.

REFLECTION

Structure didn't make me tough. It made things steadier.
The sea didn't change for me. I had to learn the physics of the deck.

Loss didn't stop anything.
It just kept moving with me—one step, one task, one day at a time. I learned that you don't have to feel ready to keep moving. You just have to be willing to handle the next logistical requirement of the day.

What stayed with me:

- You don't negotiate with the sea—you adapt to it.
- A uniform can provide the expectations you haven't yet built for yourself.
- Partnership is a trade of strengths, not an admission of weakness.

GROWTH

1.The Structure Advantage

Look at your daily habits: sleep, food, movement, or money.
Where is the loose spot causing the most friction?
What is one small, structural change you can commit to today to make things steadier?

2.The Pressure Valve

We all "push through" things just to function sometimes. But even a bridge has a load limit.
What is one thing you are currently carrying that you've been pretending doesn't have weight?
What would it look like to acknowledge that weight honestly?

3.The Lifeline

Who is the one person in your circle, personal or professional, you could ask for support right now?
What would you actually say to them?

CHAPTER 4

PIECES TO MASTERPIECE (1977–1980)

When I think about the day I was released from the army, I remember the feeling before I remember the facts. It wasn't celebration. It was exposure.

The uniform had been a kind of roof. The routine had been a kind of food. Then one day it ends. Life doesn't ask if you're ready. It just hands you responsibility.

I didn't have a soft place to fall.

A lot of soldiers traveled after the army—South America, India, Thailand. They needed to breathe, shake off what they carried, and figure out the next direction. That kind of trip was a luxury, even if no one called it that. They had families to land on. They had time to think.

My boarding school friends and I didn't have time. We didn't have extra money. We had ourselves. Outside the shelter of the

army, dinner doesn't just show up.
You plan for it.

Exposure makes you move fast.
Not because you're ungrateful, but because you have pride—and no backup.

The Extra Person

I was grateful my girlfriend's family let me sleep over. They were kind, and I knew it. But I could feel the edges. I could feel myself becoming "the extra person" in someone else's home.

That feeling is a powerful motivator. It forces you to look at the world through the lens of self-reliance. An army buddy and I started looking for a place to share in Holon.
We didn't have a car.
We had bicycles and a stubborn kind of hope.

We looked for a place close enough to work in Tel Aviv. Close enough for me to ride to Bat Yam to see my girlfriend. And cheap enough that two guys with thin pockets could survive.

The Scraper and the Paint

We found an old, rundown house· that looked like it had been forgotten for years. It had dust in layers. Doors didn't sit right. Faucets dripped like they were keeping time. Paint was peeling off the walls like it was tired of holding on.

Under all of that, there was a place trying to become a home. We rented it.

We didn't have money for "nice." We had money for basic. We scrubbed and scraped. We fixed what we could with our hands and learned the rest by trying, failing, and trying again. We replaced what was broken and patched what was usable.

There's nothing like a scraper and a few gallons of paint. They don't just cover things. They uncover you, too.

The Glazier's Lesson

We measured the broken window frames and rode our bicycles to the glazier so he could cut new panes. I remember standing at the counter, waiting. I didn't love the wait, but I was already learning something I didn't know I was learning yet.

If you don't stay close to your order, it slides to the back of the line.

In business, and in life, visibility is a form of pressure. That house renovation took about a month, long enough for it to start feeling like ours. It wasn't pretty, but it was home. At twenty-one, I had my own bedroom for the first time. I had a door that closed. I had a lock.

Privacy.

Those things sound small until you grow up without them. But I also had a wallet that was getting lighter by the moment, and the rent shows you no sympathy.

The Seed in My Pocket

My roommate found a job quickly with family, but I didn't have one yet. I could feel time tightening around me like a physical weight. So I rode my bike into Tel Aviv to look up the man who had handed me his business card months earlier, back when I was still in uniform.

His name was Moshe.
We met while he was on reserve duty at Katsor. We played soccer together, and he liked how I played. But more than that, he liked how I showed up:

On time.
Ready.
No drama.

He watched my habits the way older men watch younger men when they're deciding if you're worth trusting. Before I left, he had handed me a card and said,
"Come find me when you're out."

I kept that card in my back pocket like it was a seed.

That day, when I found Moshe at his furniture store in the industrial area of downtown Tel Aviv, he lit up like he was genuinely happy to see me. Sometimes, luck has timing. That morning, his main furniture assembly guy had quit.

Moshe had a pickup truck loaded with pieces that had to be installed at a customer's home, and the customer was waiting.
He didn't ease me into it.

He handed me an invoice, an address in Bat Yam, and the keys to the pickup truck. I looked at him and said the honest truth, "I've never assembled furniture. Are you sure?"
He waved his hands like I'd said something silly.

"Go. The customer is waiting. If you can read a soccer field, you can read parts."

That line stuck in me because it was absurd and true at the same time. There was no instruction manual. No step-by-step. No neat school system that rewarded tidy handwriting.

It was just me, the pieces, and the deadline.

In a classroom, information is flat and static. On a soccer field, information is dynamic: it moves in three dimensions. You have to track the ball, the defenders, the open space, and the clock all at once. Moshe saw that my "athletic brain" was actually a high-speed processor for spatial logic.

He wasn't hiring a carpenter.
He was hiring a problem solver.

I drove that truck to Bat Yam with a mix of nerves and adrenaline. I realized then that "experience" is often just a fancy word for having done it before. Competence is figuring it out the first time.

I started seeing the furniture as a field.
Every screw had a position; every panel had a role.

The First Real Workshop

There was a drawing on an invoice, a box of hardware that looked like mixed candy, and a pile of wood pieces that needed to become something solid in someone's living room.

I drove to Bat Yam with two feelings at once: gratitude and fear. Gratitude for the chance. Fear that I would disappoint Moshe and embarrass myself in front of a customer.

I was crossing the narrow bridge.

You cross it without seeing the full map.
You take the next true step, and then the next.
And somehow, a life starts forming under your feet.

When I arrived, I carried everything inside and spread the pieces across the living room floor. I stared at the pile and felt the reality of the task. This wasn't going to be quick. It wasn't "just assembly."

It was sequence. It was logic. It was patience.
It was the kind of intelligence school never measured.

The customer took one look at me and understood immediately that I was new. Then he did something I have never forgotten.

He sat down beside me.

No speech. No lecture. No "what kind of company is this?" Just a man who saw a young guy trying and chose kindness.

We worked through the day, and then through the night. Screws. Dowels. Pieces that only made sense after other pieces were placed first. At some point, the clock stopped mattering and it became about one thing: Finishing.

It was 4:00 a.m. when we finally stood back and looked at the finished piece.

I drove Moshe's truck home with my eyelids half open. I didn't feel heroic; I felt human. I felt relieved. I felt proud in a quiet way that didn't need applause.

That customer's check closed the job, and his kindness opened my future. Today, after all this time, I've forgotten his name and address, but I am and always will be deeply grateful for his compassion.

You don't always know the impact small acts of kindness and compassion can make in another's life.

The Invisible Glue

I walked into Moshe's store the next morning with the payment in my hand and my eyes half alive. He nodded like a man whose expectations had been met. He wasn't emotional about it; he was steady.

"You see?" he said. "You CAN use soccer strategy for other things."

From that day on, I became his main assembly guy. One person, a toolbox, and a willingness to figure it out. I entered home after home assembling wardrobes, cabinets, desks, children's rooms, and TV units that made living rooms feel complete.

Every home had its smell; coffee, laundry detergent, lemon cleaner, baby cream, or cumin cooking in the kitchen while I worked in the other room.

I started to understand something about furniture that surprised me. It isn't just wood—it is a gathering point. It's where a family sits, eats, argues, and relaxes.

When you assemble something in a home, you aren't just
building an object.
You're helping a life settle into place.

And there's a kind of invisible glue in those moments. Compassion is the glue you can't see, but you feel. This is where sequence, patience, and responsibility became real to me in a way school never did.

It taught me that my dyslexia did not decide my future. It simply pushed me into a lane where my gifts worked better than words. I could see how things fit; I could picture the finished piece before it existed. I could solve with my hands and my head together.

I didn't get that job because of a diploma.
I got it because of how I showed up.

A clean fix is better than a hidden flaw. Piece by piece, it will all come together.

After about a year, I felt the next pull—that feeling has followed me my whole life. When I learn a system, I start wanting to build my own.

I had saved a little money. I had confidence now. Not the loud kind, but real confidence; the kind you get from doing hard things repeatedly until they stop being scary.

I didn't want to compete with Moshe. I respected him and I didn't forget where my first chance came from.
I just wanted to see what I could build on my own.

The Return to Jerusalem

I decided to take my next step far away from the comforts of Tel Aviv. I went back to the place where I had first learned to walk six miles a day.

Jerusalem.

The city had not changed, but I had.

I wasn't the boy with a hole in his boot anymore; I was a man with a toolbox and a plan.

I searched the streets until I found exactly what I needed: a modest storefront with enough space to build and a tiny, converted garage studio for a bed.

I took them both. To make it happen, I had to reach into my pockets and pull out everything I had saved.
I emptied my savings to buy my future.

This wasn't a fantasy. It wasn't a "dream" I hoped would come true.

It was a calculated risk built on a foundation of skills I had already earned in the real world. I knew how to load a truck. I knew how to assemble a wardrobe. I knew how to talk to a customer until 4:00 a.m.

I wasn't betting on luck.
I was betting on my own ability to show up.

In 1978, at the age of twenty-two, I officially opened the doors to my first business: Custom Furniture & Shelves, Ltd.
The sign above the door was simple, but seeing my own company's name in print felt like a different kind of uniform. It didn't belong to the Navy or a school system.
It belonged to me.

First Day: Freedom With Conditions

The first morning I unlocked the shop, the key turned like it was asking me a question.

The space was small, with a bare floor and a fresh paint smell. Outside, the street kept moving like nothing special was happening, but inside, something was. It felt like a different kind of freedom.

The kind with conditions.

Freedom—with rent.
Freedom—with permits.
Freedom—with a phone that could ring or stay silent all day.

I stood there for a second, watching and listening to the quiet. It wasn't a peaceful quiet; it was a "working quiet." It was the kind that echoes. You wanted your own door—now you have to become the man who can hold it.

It's not a dream.
It's a furnace.

Pressure doesn't always break you.
Sometimes it compresses you into something stronger.
That's what diamonds are: Carbon that didn't quit.

And I didn't quit.

I bought floor samples from carpenters in Tel Aviv. They believed in me enough to give me ninety days to pay, secretly cheering for me in their own way. I assembled them until displays filled the space. They leaned against the wall, waiting to be chosen.

I laid my pencil, ruler, and tape measure on the counter like tools on an altar. Not spiritual. Practical.

I ran an ad in the local paper, hung a banner, and put balloons outside, because people recognize color before they recognize words.

Then I wrote a promise:

Design your own bookshelf, wardrobe, desk, children's room.
Best price.
100% guarantee.
Pay when assembled.

I added my picture next to my logo, because I wanted customers to know who would walk into their home.

People don't just buy furniture.
They buy the feeling of a future taking shape.

First Day: First Order

Pressure showed up right on time.

A woman walked in with two kids. She arrived the way real customers always come—busy, direct, and completely uninterested in my dreams.

She didn't care about my "new start."
She only cared if I could solve a problem in her life.

She looked around, touched a sample shelf, and asked one question that every homeowner has:

"Can you do this without making my house a mess?"

I smiled and nodded like I had done it forever.
Inside, my chest was loud.
This was the moment where you find out if your business is real or just a story you tell yourself to feel better about being broke.

I sketched and watched her eyes more than the drawing on the paper.

In sales, and in life, you have to believe the room, not the drawing. When she finally looked at the sketch, nodded, and said, "Yes. That's it," I felt a sensation like a click in a lock.

She left a down payment for two desks, with bookcases and matching chairs.

It was the first money I earned under my own sign. After she left, I sat down and stared at that receipt like it was proof I existed.

Momentum starts like that.
Quiet.
Then all at once.

The Discipline of Craft

I learned quickly that the strongest business skill isn't talking. It is listening. I would tweak a sketch until I saw the customer's shoulders drop and their eyes say, "Yes, that's the one." Once the "deal" was sealed in their mind, I'd break it into exact measurements and send the order to carpenters in Tel Aviv to produce.

Words were still a struggle for me. Long paragraphs were never my friends. So I did what worked: arrows, numbers, simple drawings, and clear sequences.

I didn't need a vocabulary.
I needed a process.

And I learned rules:
Believe the room, not the drawing.
Kindness is the tool that isn't in the box.

The religious community became some of my best customers. They wanted strong, beautiful cabinets to hold holy books. I understood that world because I had grown up in it. They appreciated good work, they paid fairly, and when they trusted you, they told everyone they knew.
Trust travels faster than advertising.

When you listen first, you build right.
When you build right, you don't have to sell hard.
The work speaks for you.

Running a shop taught me the same lesson the market taught me, just in a different outfit: price honestly, show up when you said you would, and promise a day late so you can finish a day early.

That's how you protect the middle of every job.
The handoff between plan and delivery is where most things fall apart.

I kept the rule that I had learned years earlier in the bread factory:
Tight, not fast.
Precision over fear.
But then Israel did what Israel does: it gave me pride and pressure at the same time.

Permits moved slow. Regulations came with surprises. And reserve duty did not ask permission. Sometimes the army drafts you right in the middle of your best momentum, and you are expected to show up.

One day, while loading my truck, I got the call.
It wasn't a request. It was a demand.

I was being drafted for reserves, and this time, they needed my truck too. In an instant, the physics of my business disappeared.

Now the math changed.

The Friction of Duty

No truck meant no installs. No installs meant delays. Delays meant reputation damage.

My truck was already loaded to the brim with parts. My head was prepared with the sequence of the job:
Install.
Finish clean.
Collect payment.
Move to the next job.

I drove to the customer anyway, tools rattling in the back. I knocked on the door and when he answered I told him the truth: "I've been called in. I have to report now. They're taking my truck."

You could see disappointment on his face, but you could also see understanding. That's Israel. People complain, then they adjust, because everyone knows the rules of the country we live in.

I promised to call him first thing when I returned. I promised to make it right. Then I did the only thing I could do:
I returned to my shop, unloaded the truck, and hung a sign in my window:
"Drafted to army reserves. I'll be back."

Customers were patient, they understood. But the backlog didn't. Orders stacked up. Delivery dates slid. And I started to feel trapped in a system that didn't leave room for a small business to breathe.

The Wall

That's when the old dream started knocking again.

America.

Not because I wanted to leave Israel; I loved my country. But love doesn't remove obstacles. Sometimes you can love a place and still know it's not the place where your next chapter grows. When pressure builds with no release, you start hearing yourself more clearly.

I knew I had to move on. And moving on had a price.

My girlfriend wanted marriage. She wanted us to build a life in Israel, the normal way. When I told her about America, she didn't play games with me. She told me straight:

"If you leave, we're finished."

That sentence was a wall that I stood in front of for a while.

The Cost of Growth

Some choices don't come as right or wrong.
They come as loss.

You choose, and something breaks either way.

I knew something about myself even then. If I didn't take the chance, I would carry regret like a stone for the rest of my life. I didn't want to hurt her, but I couldn't shrink my life to avoid guilt. I wasn't going to let fear negotiate me out of my future.

After one year of building a successful business from nothing, I sold everything. The stock. The tools. The truck that had become my partner on every delivery. I turned my physical assets back into the liquid capital I needed for the next leap.

I chose growth; I carried the cost.
I shook hands with the people who had watched me build myself from scratch—the vendors who gave me credit and the customers who gave me trust. Then I locked the shop door for the last time.

One door closed.
Another opened into a wide, unfamiliar sky.
I was twenty-three years old.
I was heading to America.

TREE WISDOM

These were the trunk years.
The roots held. The work became real.

Sequence.
Patience.
Trust.

To build without instructions is to grow like a tree—reaching higher because the ground underneath is solid. Some builds are decisions. They require leaving one soil behind to grow in another. Piece by piece, the trunk learns it can hold weight.

REFLECTION

Freedom came with conditions: rent, promises, and delivery dates. I learned that you don't just "get" freedom. You maintain it through the quality of your output.
Trust was built the same way as the furniture. It was step by step. It was clean. There was nothing hidden.

In business, and in life, your reputation is the invisible glue that holds the whole structure together.

What stayed with me:

- You don't need a manual if you understand the logic of the parts.
- Reliability is the only currency that doesn't devalue.
- Sometimes growth comes with a price that is hard to pay.

GROWTH

1.Building Without a Map

Where in your life are you currently building something without a set of instructions?
What tools do you already have that you haven't started using?

2.The Price of the Transplant

Moving to a "new soil" usually means leaving something behind. What is the one thing you are afraid to let go of, even though you know your current "pot" is too small for your roots?

CHAPTER 5

TRANSPLANTED: AMERICAN SOIL (1980–1983)

Crossing the Ocean

I was twenty-three when I boarded my first airplane. Eleven hours later, I landed in New York City.

I carried one small suitcase and one backpack. Inside them were some clothes. Inside me were two loud feelings that didn't want to share the same space: the excitement for what was ahead, and the ache of leaving people that I loved behind.

The moment I stepped off the plane, I realized I had skipped over my most important main tool.

Language.

The airport smelled like coffee, jet fuel, and the warm breath of thousands of strangers moving in every direction at once. The announcements repeated in English, and I understood almost nothing. Not "a little."

Almost nothing.

In that moment, I wasn't an entrepreneur.
I was a traveler without a map.

I could guess "Exit," "Baggage," and "Taxi," the icons helped. Icons are universal. They speak to the physics of the room. But the words were a lock I didn't have the key to.

It hit me in a sharp, cold way: I had crossed an ocean to live in a country where I barely spoke the language. My chest tightened. Not panic. Just the quiet realization that nothing around me would adjust for me.

Motion vs. Meaning

My relationship with school didn't prepare me for a country built on words I didn't understand. I wasn't the kid who sat and did homework. I was the kid who found a way out of the classroom and into movement.

But in New York, motion wasn't enough.

Now I had to survive inside a language. I would have to learn to get by. And I would have to learn fast.

Outside, taxis slid past like yellow fish in a fast river. I didn't have the money to live freely. I had crossed an ocean, not won a lottery, so I chose to ride the train to Long Island. It was the most economical choice at the time.

Economics often dictates the first step of any journey.

It was winter, real winter. The kind that makes your ears sting and turns your breath into a little chimney you can't shut off. I was quickly learning the first American rule: Everything moves fast in New York except nature.

Nature takes its time, like it's trying to tell us something.

I told myself the cold in my bones was only weather, not fear.
That's the thing about starting over.
Your body doesn't know the difference at first.

Cold feels like fear.
Silence feels like failure.

I sat on that train and watched the grey landscape of New York roll by. Everything looked the same, and nothing felt familiar.

The Soft Landing

Family on my father's side offered me their basement guest room so I could get my footing. I made the connection before I bought my ticket. I wanted a softer landing.

They were kind people and busy people, the house pulsing with small children, schedules, and a life that already had its shape. I was truly grateful.

But I hadn't crossed an ocean to live on someone else's schedule.

I needed my own space, even if it was small, even if it was ugly. A man can be grateful and still know he needs a door that is his. That line drew itself clearly in my head. I couldn't unsee it.

Ten minutes down the street from their house was a pizza place that became my daily comfort. I could smell the hot slices before I even turned the corner, the aroma drifting down the street like it was calling my name. New York pizza is the best. I've always wondered why; maybe the city's hunger is part of the recipe.

The Cost of Comfort

That pizza place became my hangout, and little by little I depleted the money I had brought with me from Israel. Every slice reminded me I wasn't working. And every day that passed made that louder. I knew I would have to find a job soon if I wanted to make it in New York and live the dream I had carried across the ocean.

New Yorkers asked me where I was from, and when I replied, "Jerusalem," they nodded like that explained everything.

Religion.
War.
Politics.

They handed me their assumptions like a coat and expected me to wear it. I didn't have time to contemplate any of it. I was trying to survive.

The Miracle in Brooklyn

One afternoon, sitting with my slice, I met an Israeli man who lived in Brooklyn. Hearing him speak Hebrew felt like drinking water after being thirsty without noticing it. We talked, and within minutes he gave me advice that still feels like a miracle.

He told me I should move to Brighton Beach. Rent was cheaper, and he knew of a room for one hundred dollars a month.

One hundred dollars.

That number sounded like a rope thrown down to help you climb higher.

He was leaving in an hour, and he said he would take me there if I wanted.

I didn't hesitate. Waiting wasn't part of my system.
Some offers are not "maybe."

Some offers are a door.
You walk through—or you stay staring at the wall.

The Sign

I ran back to my family's place. I packed my backpack and small suitcase, thanked them for their kindness, and told them I was moving to Brooklyn. It was a fast exit, but in New York, fast is the only speed that works.

I raced back to the pizza place, almost out of breath, and was relieved to see the man was still there. He had waited for me.

In a city of eight million people, one man waiting feels like a sign.

The train ride was about an hour and a half. Along the way, he gave me advice like an older brother: practical and direct. He told me to look for work near King's Highway because there were many Jewish families there. It would be easier for me to get by with limited English.

He was teaching me how to find my "calibration" in a new system.

The Russian Landlord

He even told me what to say to the Russian landlord so she would rent the room to me.
"Tell her you're good with your hands. Tell her you can fix anything she needs in the house."

I smiled.
I could fix anything she needed. I had been fixing things my whole life.

Not always perfect.
But enough to keep things standing.

In business, and in survival, you don't sell what you *can't* do. You sell the one thing you *can* do better than anyone else. I didn't have a credit score or a local reference, but I had a toolbox in my brain and a willingness to trade labor for a roof.

I wasn't asking for a room.
I was proposing a partnership.

The Basement Window

When we arrived, he walked with me, introduced me to the lady, and helped me secure the room. It was underground in a basement with a narrow bed, a small dresser, and a partial window that looked out onto a parking lot.

My view was car tires and people's ankles passing by.

I had slept on floors most of my life, so the basement didn't insult me.

It gave me what I needed: my own space, a door, and a corner of the world that was mine. Ten minutes from the beach for one hundred dollars a month.

I shared a kitchen and bathroom with two other tenants. It wasn't much. But it was enough to begin.

We were all just getting by. One roommate spent his days walking the beach with his "magic stick," searching for gold and jewelry like the sea was going to reward him. The other drifted through life without ambition, and I always felt something fragile in him, something that made the world harder to carry.

The house had the kind of mismatched kitchen you invent in your twenties: two mugs, four forks, plates that didn't match, and a pan that might have been older than all of us combined. The refrigerator hummed like it was tired but still trying. The hallway smelled like boiled cabbage, laundry detergent, and sometimes someone's dinner sneaking under the door.

It didn't bother me.

I pressed my forehead to the small mirror and told myself the words that had carried me since I was a boy staring at a blank school page.

Start.
Keep going.
You will arrive.

I didn't need motivation. I needed direction.

New Language of Measurement

Brighton Beach had its own language: Russian delis selling smoked fish and black bread, pickled everything, and little shops with gold jewelry in the window. A boardwalk that led into the long horizon of Coney Island. Trains rattling above like a metronome.

The first American lesson wasn't only language. It was measurements.

Israel measures in centimeters. Here, it was inches and fractions.

Three-eighths. Five-sixteenths. A hair under a half. The tape measure looked simple until you tried to cut a board on a windy balcony and realized you were living in a system built out of tiny slices.

I made myself a little cheat sheet on a thin scrap of wood. I kept it in my pocket until my hands remembered.

In business, and in a new country, you don't fight the system of measurement. You learn the fractions until you can speak them with your eyes closed. Precision doesn't care about your native tongue; it only cares about the fit.

Opportunity In Flames

Work came the old way: by word of mouth. A guy knew a guy who needed hands to clean up after restaurant fires. The work was dirty and urgent, and it didn't care that my English wasn't pretty.

When he said "fire cleanup," something inside me paused.

In Israel, the army had given me a role that fit. I didn't just fight fires; I trained others to do it. You don't argue with fire. You read it, move with it, and act.

Now I was in America, barely able to form a sentence in English, and my first real job was walking into burned restaurants.

Life has a strange sense of humor. It doesn't always give you something new. Sometimes it gives you the same thing in a different place.

The flames were gone, but the work was the same.
Sequence.
Patience.
No panic.

Smoke damage doesn't require perfect grammar; it requires movement. We arrived early to find tile walls streaked with soot, like gray tears, and ovens coughing black. Grease had been blown into places it never should have reached.

Tight, not fast.

I scraped and hauled and scrubbed until my tongue went numb from chemicals and my arms felt like they belonged to someone else.

The kitchen equipment had opinions. Heavy ones. You measure hallways. You measure stairs. You measure the stubbornness of a banister.

Sometimes you lift a piece like a stretcher and breathe on a count.

One, two, step.

Staircase Logic

New York taught me to think like a staircase.
Tight corners. No hero moves. No dropped edge.
In a city built on old stone and narrow hallways, nothing is ever perfectly straight.

You learn to respect the angle.

On Sundays, I gave my feet a small rest and my spirit a little room. I rode the subway wherever the map looked interesting, eating cheap food made by people who worked as hard to make it as I worked to afford it.
A dollar slice that folded in half.
A bagel that fought back.
Coffee in a paper cup that burned your mouth and woke your bones.

Then Monday came; and with it, the truth of survival. Early mornings. Long days. Whatever job was available.

One day, the boss told us to throw away "junk,"—burnt equipment from a restaurant that had gone up in flames. I looked at the pile and saw something different.

It wasn't junk.

I saw machines that were dirty but still alive. I saw stainless counters with years of service left in them. Freezers. Ovens. This was equipment that could be cleaned, repaired, and resold.

By then, I had learned the ropes and taken notes along the way. I made phone calls I wasn't told to make. I found a buyer I wasn't supposed to find.

I turned trash into five thousand dollars.

I thought it would make me more valuable. I thought it would prove I could see opportunities others missed. I expected a handshake, maybe a bonus, or at least a nod of respect. That's how I understood effort back then.

Instead, it made me dangerous.

The Final Handshake

My boss fired me for being "too smart." I didn't argue. I understood exactly what he meant.
It was the shortest, most honest performance review I've ever had.

He didn't want an innovator; he wanted someone who stayed within the lines. I was coloring outside of them, and I was doing it faster than he was. In a rigid system, initiative is often mistaken for a threat.

I walked out with five thousand dollars in my pocket and a hard lesson instead of a steady paycheck.

At twenty-three, in a city that didn't know my name, that trade felt exactly right. With that cash, I wasn't just "rich" for a moment; I was independent. I had the capital to say no to the wrong jobs so I could wait for the right ones.

Money measures choices; it doesn't just measure hours.

When you only have a paycheck, you are a passenger in someone else's vehicle. When you have capital, you have the keys. I was learning the most important rule of the American market:

The more you own your process, the less you have to sell your time.

The Red Pontiac Years

With five hundred of those dollars, I bought a Red Pontiac station wagon. It was loud and honest.

It wasn't a dream car.
It was a tool.

It gave me range. It gave me weekends. It gave me a way to keep moving when the city tried to trap me in one neighborhood. I drove up to flea markets, the kind where wind pushed through the aisles like it paid admission.

I met an Israeli American couple selling women's clothing. They saw me hustling in the cold and invited me over. That conversation rolled into Friday night, Shabbat dinner, in their home.

The soup tasted familiar.

Familiar food does something to a man who is far from home. It softens the edges of loneliness for a few hours and reminded me of my roots, and that I still belong.

That night, they offered me a partnership on a stand upstate. I said yes.

I didn't have cushions.
I had hunger dressed like ambition.

The route was brutal: two hours each way from Brighton Beach. But I was grateful for my Red Pontiac and the work. The market gave me just enough to keep moving.

Not enough to sit down.

The Bronx Lesson

When sales slowed and covering rent became a challenge, I didn't wait for the floor to drop. I asked my partners for introductions. They connected me to a man with a chain of unisex discount clothing stores on Delancey Street, on the Lower East Side of Manhattan.

I interviewed. I got hired as security.

It was dangerous work.
I carried a baseball bat and protected the inventory from theft, and I moved heavy boxes to stock the shelves between the moments of friction. After a couple of months, they transferred me to a larger area, an area that lived by a different set of rules: The Bronx.

The streets there had a weight to them. Crime was a constant hum. Gangs. Drug dealers. A permanent, low-grade static in the air that tells you your back should have eyes.

In the Bronx, the "Physics of the Room" became the "Physics of the Street."

I wasn't afraid in the way people imagine fear. I had grown up watching corners in Jerusalem. I knew how to read the shift in a man's shoulders before it became a punch.

I confronted men who were trying to get by any way they could—stealing and cheating—and I learned quickly that survival has a way of pulling values into a fight.

If love and safety aren't in your top values because you don't have them, you start building your identity around endurance.

One day, someone loosened the lug nuts on my front tires while I was inside the store. I didn't know it at first. I only felt the shaking while I drove. It was a metallic wobble that tells your body something is wrong before your mind can even name the vibration in the steering wheel.

I pulled over just in time. Both front tires were loose, nearly disassembled. If I had been driving fast, I wouldn't have made it to the next corner.

Sometimes survival is a bridge you cross in the dark.
Only in the morning do you name it courage.

After that incident, I didn't just walk to my car. I began checking my tires every single time I left for home. I learned that in business, and in survival, the "small parts" you take for granted are usually the ones that can do damage.

Vigilance isn't paranoia.
It is quality control for your own life.

When Responsibility Arrives

All that time, I kept in touch with my first love by writing letters. There were no emails, and long-distance phone calls were a luxury we couldn't afford.

So we wrote.

How she read my chicken-scratch handwriting, I still don't know, but we stayed connected through paper and patience.

When she graduated, we were eager to see each other. I bought her airline ticket and arranged for her to stay with me in the basement. I didn't want to be alone anymore and I was relieved that she agreed.

When she arrived, the basement didn't feel like a basement. It felt like a home because there was someone to share it with. I even helped her get a job near me, working as a cashier.

It felt like a breath of fresh air to have her with me.

The Reward: The Brown Camaro

The Red Pontiac had served its purpose; it was a survival vehicle for a survival season. But as the work in the Bronx began to take hold and my girlfriend entered the picture, the "rhythm of just getting by" wasn't enough anymore. I needed a symbol of the new direction and a more reliable means of transportation.

I traded the Red Pontiac for a Brown Camaro.

It wasn't about the engine. It was about the oxygen. I bought it for me, but I drove it for her. It was my way of saying the basement season was over.

When you spend your life building a trunk through discipline, there eventually comes a moment when you have to let the branches reach. The Brown Camaro was my first branch.

But after six more months in that dangerous work, I knew I needed something more secure. It wasn't just me anymore. Responsibility changes shape when love enters the room.

You stop thinking only about what you can survive.
You start thinking about what you can build.

Word of mouth led me back to a familiar lane: Furniture assembly.

I took side jobs with an assembly company. I knew this work. I trusted my hands. I trusted my ability to solve what didn't come with instructions.

And then, through the grapevine, a businessman from Brooklyn sought me out. He had heard I specialized in furniture assembly, and he had an idea.

He wanted to expand to California.

The Decision

Word has reached him about the open opportunities on the West Coast for customized furniture. Because of my reputation, he offered me a basic salary plus a percentage of profit. It wasn't a fantasy offer; it was a real door.

A door with hinges that could hold weight.

I looked at my life in that moment. I looked at the basement window and the miles I had put on the old, Red Pontiac that paved the way for the Brown Camaro. I looked at her, finally standing there beside me, and the constant "what's next" that never got quiet.

The Bronx had taught me how to survive.
Now, I wanted to learn how to build.

When opportunity comes knocking, you don't ask it to wait while you get comfortable. You don't tell it to come back when the timing is better.

You open the door and let it in.

This wasn't just a job offer; it was a relocation of my entire future. That was the next true step. I didn't need more information. I needed to move.

And it was going to change everything.

TREE WISDOM

When a tree is transplanted, growth pauses.
The roots search quietly before the branches rise again.

These were transplant years.

The roots did not disappear; they were lifted, wrapped, and carried across an ocean. In new soil, roots test the ground before drinking. Branches hold still until the wind introduces itself.

The trunk thickened in a different climate: snow on the bark, steam from the street, and light from windows stacked to the sky.

A graft took: old discipline meeting new opportunity.

The heartwood stayed the same.
The tree learned a new climate.

REFLECTION

America didn't hand me a new life. It handed me a new set of rules. I had to learn them fast. I learned that comfort is expensive, and so is hesitation.

Small kindnesses can change a whole future.

I saw that in the man at the pizza shop who waited for me to pack my bags so he could show me a way into Brooklyn. Without that one hour of his time, my path would have looked completely different.

I also learned that survival can pull you into a fight if you don't protect your values. In the Bronx, I learned that vigilance isn't paranoia; it is quality control for your own life. Most of all, I learned that the same sentence that saved me as a boy still saves me as a man:

Start.
Keep going.
You will arrive.

I didn't need guarantees. I needed movement.

GROWTH

1.The Language Gap

In New York, I was limited because I couldn't speak the language.

What is the one area—skill, communication, or money— where you currently feel "limited"?

What is the first tiny lesson you can learn this week to start bridging that gap?

2.The Basement Window

Sometimes a view of a parking lot and passing ankles is the exact foothold you need to begin. A small space with a narrow view, but one that is entirely yours.

Where in your life are you currently in a "basement season"?

What is that season giving you that a "penthouse view" couldn't?

3.The Gratitude Ledger

Who belongs on your gratitude ledger right now?
What is one simple thank-you you can offer this week?

CHAPTER 6

CALIFORNIA DREAMING (1983–1985)

Three Thousand Miles, Three Days

Later that year in 1983, after several months of planning and mapping out the venture like it was a new kind of chessboard, I said yes.

I packed the Brown Camaro with a small duffel, a box of tools, and a paper map that folded the wrong way, no matter how politely you asked it.

Three thousand miles in three days. It sounds like a lot, but when you have a dream in the trunk and a partner in the passenger seat, the miles move differently.

Behind me lay the Red Pontiac seasons—the years of "just enough" and "almost there." In front of me was a three-day sprint into a life I hadn't yet earned. The Brown Camaro wasn't just a car; it was a promise that I was finally moving at the speed of my own ambition.

My love stayed in Brooklyn, safe in the basement room we knew, while I went first to test the ground. I told myself it was temporary. That made it easier to leave. Risk should take the primary stakeholders first. We promised calls on Sundays and letters on the days when money did not let us call.

America is bigger than a plan.

Pennsylvania was trees and truck lights like beads on a string.
Ohio was long, flat, and honest.
Somewhere after Missouri the sky widened, like it needed more room to think.
New Mexico smelled like dust and pine.
Arizona was a red movie I had not paid for.

Three thousand miles is a long time to think.

My partner and I turned the Brown Camaro into a boardroom at eighty miles an hour. We didn't talk about the scenery; we talked about drayage and assembly times. We were moving a life, but calculating a venture.

By the time we hit the Arizona desert the plan was as tight as the lug nuts on the wheels.
We ate at places with names that sounded like they were invented that morning. Coffee that could melt a spoon. Eggs that arrived fast and hot. We slept in motor inns where the ice machine never had ice and the carpet told stories I did not ask to hear.

The road gave me simple rules:

Start early.
Fuel before the light goes on.
Stretch your back when you pump gas.
Thank the clerk.
Keep moving.

Three days later, we hit Los Angeles air—damp, sweet, and tired of itself. Freeways braided and unbraided like somebody kept changing their mind.

We were not dreaming anymore. We were arriving.

Long Beach: Testing the Ground

Long Beach smelled like salt and exhaust. It offered what we needed.

It wasn't a city that asked for your resume; it was a city that asked for your hands. It was grit and logistics. It was the smell of a port that never slept and a freeway that didn't care where you were going, as long as you kept moving.

Long Beach was close enough to Los Angeles to matter, but far enough to afford.

The warehouse we found had a roll-up door that jumped if you pulled too hard, a concrete floor with paint ghosts from other tenants, and one small office with a crooked window.

The rent did not leave room for mistakes. It didn't forgive them either.

It left just enough for a used pallet jack, a broom, and a cheap coffee maker that hissed like a hostile cat.

My partner had already shipped a container of furniture from his factory in Israel. Knock-down systems and display units. This was the language my hands already spoke. He bought us a typewriter, too, which was an excellent idea because its steel-struck letters were more legible than my own handwriting.

He shook my hand like we had already won. Then he flew back to New York.

I drove him to Los Angeles Airport and watched him disappear into the crowd with his backpack and his confidence. I stayed behind with the warehouse and the calendar. And just like that, it was my responsibility.

Standing in that empty warehouse for the first time was different than the Bronx. In New York, the space felt cramped and heavy with the past. Here, the emptiness felt like an invitation. I remember walking the perimeter, my boots echoing off the concrete. I wasn't fitting into someone else's system. I was the system.

The Warehouse That Couldn't Be Lazy

I built a calendar that couldn't be lazy. In business, if you don't set the pace, the day sets it for you.

For the first couple of weeks, I slept in the warehouse and showered at a nearby gym. Mornings, I cleaned—sweeping dust into piles like I could sweep away my own fear. Afternoons, I went out looking for buyers. Cold calls. Knocking. Asking. At night, I called Brooklyn. I told her about the sea fog that rolled over the freeway like a blanket, about sunsets that looked fake until they didn't. I told her there was real work here, and that I wanted her with me.

The Brown Camaro was for the arrival, but the warehouse growth needed bigger. I added a U-Haul truck and an old yellow forklift to match it—both worn, both reliable in their own way and somehow it all fit.

That's when I ran into a system nobody warns you about: the DMV. Titles, plates, lines that didn't move and rules that did—the kind of place where time disappears if you let it. I learned quickly that a clerk can save you three weeks of your life by caring for thirty seconds. So I didn't show up hoping for a break. I showed up ready—copies, originals, a pen that worked, and a specific kind of patience.

The guard looked at my stack of papers and said, "You came prepared."
I looked back at him and said, "I can't afford to come twice."

Showroom Out of Dust

The first shipment arrived.

I assembled until my fingers went numb from screwing pieces together, or until the cordless drill went soft and needed the charger's mercy.

I built the first display wall in the warehouse to show the line.

No one buys a sketch. People buy what they can see and touch.

I leveled every shelf until the bubble sat dead center. I tapped the shims like a drummer who knew the beat. I wrote prices on blue painter's tape. I swept again. I opened the roll-up door and let the light in.

If something isn't square, it never stays quiet.
It will scream at you later. So I kept fixing things early.

Small.
Clean.
Honest.

This was the first moment the business felt real.

By noon, sweat drew a line down my back and the music from a taquería on the corner cut through the warehouse like a friendly knife. I learned my new city by taste. Breakfast burritos wrapped like gifts. Donuts at six in the morning that felt like apology and welcome at the same time. Extra hot cortados that kept my eyes open when paperwork tried to close them.

The One-Way Ticket

I finally found an apartment that would suit us, and I sent my girlfriend a one-way ticket to California. We were both so happy when she arrived. The palm trees and weather reminded us of Israel, but with a calm vibe—a West Coast rhythm we were both ready to learn.

We didn't have much, so settling in didn't take much time. We didn't need "much." We just needed a foothold. We began to work together, side by side, building the branches of life we had only discussed over the phone.

Lakewood: The First Verdict

Our first sale was to a family-owned furniture store in Lakewood.

I priced fair. She nodded once, like a judge who already had the verdict.

On install day, I didn't just show up; I arrived with a system. I laid moving blankets, taped corners, and worked tight instead of fast.

The Long Beach

By the end of summer, a showroom stood where dust had been.

It wasn't a miracle. It was a series of small, tight decisions that held weight.

Four months later, the Brown Camaro was still in the driveway, but a 24-foot truck was doing the heavy lifting now. My partner was back in New York, and calls from Brooklyn were my only anchor. But the work was moving. The warehouse floor didn't have ghosts anymore; it had inventory.

When Momentum Arrives

"Do the small things like they carry the house, because they do."

One month after the Lakewood delivery, the rhythm shifted. I hired my first two full-time commission-based employees to help with sales. The office work, sales, invoices, and payments stayed my job along with my girlfriend. I was no longer a solo operator; I was a lead. But in those days, a lead didn't sit in an office. I would load, I would deliver, and I would assemble.

I was doing everything at once.

I was learning that you should never confuse doing it alone with doing it yourself. There is a difference between being a loner and being a leader. One keeps you small, and the other builds you.

Piece by piece, it stopped being a warehouse and started being a showroom.

The Corkboard Audit

In the early stages of expansion, the percentage only appears after costs are stripped away and costs like to multiply when you stop watching.

I made an office corkboard out of a wall to hold pinned receipts by week and invoices by stage.

If the numbers aren't visible, they aren't real.

Work began to stack up. Referrals started to flow like the tide. The first six months we concentrated on Long Beach and Los Angeles. And then expanded to Orange County.

I kept a ledger with three columns, just like I had in the Bronx, but the stakes were higher:

1. Materials.
2. Time.
3. Gratitude.

The Architecture of Trust

Independent stores across Los Angeles flipped through my photocopied catalog and pointed to the pages they wanted. My showroom had a system. I priced fair, delivered on time, and fixed what wasn't right without debate.

The city answered with orders.

Before the year was up, I hired one driver and one assembly helper. I was learning a fundamental American rule: do the job until it is too big to do alone, then keep doing the part that only you can do.

Design.
Quality.
The handshake that turns to trust.
That was the new currency.

The Future Walks In

My girlfriend would bring lunch to the warehouse. For the first time, the future felt like more than a solo mission. It didn't just feel earned; it felt shared. We built our routines in this new city the same way I built the furniture. One piece at a time. Tight. Square. No shortcuts.

Then my world shifted again.

She told me we were going to have a baby.

For a second I didn't speak. It wasn't because I wasn't happy. It was because the feeling was too big for my mouth. My mind did what it always does when something sacred appears; it ran the whole film at once.

I saw the basement window in Brooklyn.
I felt the cold warehouse floor in Long Beach.
I remembered the Motel 6 nights and the
first display wall I leveled until it finally behaved.
And now, a life was coming.

I had built my whole life around:
Start.
    Keep going.
        You will arrive.

But a baby is different. A baby doesn't care about your business play or your shipping schedules. A baby only asks one question: *Will you be there?*

The New Equation

The showroom lights reflected in her eyes, and I understood a new equation.

Success isn't numbers first.
It's faces first.

I had spent my life learning how to build things that last. Now I had to learn if I could build a family while I was busy building our future income. My mind ran the numbers, but the math of fatherhood didn't work like the math of furniture.

I worked. I worked until the sun was a memory and my hands were stained with the dust of a dozen different woods. I brought home the money. I brought home the riches of life and the security I never had in the basement. I thought a full bank account was the same thing as a full heart.

I was a provider, but I was still learning how to be a father.

I didn't know yet that you can't buy back the hours you spend at the warehouse. I didn't know that being there is a different kind of "tight and square" than assembling a wall. I was building a future for a child I hadn't met, but I was doing it by being somewhere else.

The Brown Camaro was fast, but it couldn't be in two places at once.

The Circle Closes

Before the baby arrived, we went back.

We flew across the ocean to Israel to get married in a big wedding. It was a celebration that felt like a victory lap for everything we had survived. Standing there, surrounded by family and the air of my childhood, the distance between the Jerusalem sun and the Long Beach port felt shorter than it ever had before.

The wedding was loud, filled with music, heavy food, and the kind of joy that only comes when people see you've made it. I stood there in a suit that didn't feel like a uniform, looking at my wife, knowing we were carrying a new life back to the West Coast.

We had the blessing. We had the history. Now, we had to go back and finish the build.

People imagine change arriving with trumpets. Most of the time it slips in like a carpenter you trust.
Quiet.
Exact.
On schedule.

The Architecture of Absence

We returned to California and the pace didn't just pick up; it exploded.

The baby was coming, and my reaction was to work harder. I was driven by a specific kind of fear, the fear of the basement window. I didn't want my child to ever see the world from the level of someone else's ankles.
So I stayed at the warehouse.

I brought home the money. I brought home the riches of life. I made sure the house was solid, the fridge was full, and the future was funded. I was a provider, but I was doing it from a distance.

I thought fatherhood was a project you could fund. I didn't realize yet that while I was leveling the shelves for other people's homes, my own house was waiting for me to just sit down.

I was building a kingdom for a child I hadn't met, but I was doing it by being somewhere else. I was a great businessman, but I was still an apprentice at being a father.

Believe the Room

New York gave me grit. California gave me scale.

The boy who slept on floors, now built rooms for other people's lives. The man who had spent his youth guarding doors started opening them. The same instincts that once read a soccer match on a dirt field in Jerusalem now helped me read streets, leases, neighborhoods, and the invisible current running through a city.

Intuition became my due diligence.

If the room felt right, I trusted it. Then I checked the numbers to keep the trust honest. But even in the high-speed rhythm of the Brown Camaro and the growing fleet of trucks, I was learning a new kind of gravity.

There were hard business lessons tucked inside the good months.

TREE WISDOM

These were my branch years.

My roots were still deep in the Jerusalem soil, and my trunk had hardened through the winters of New York. But California was giving the tree room to spread its branches wider. I was learning that sunlight alone does not grow a tree. Structure does. Repetition does. Showing up when no one is watching does.

And when new life begins forming, the tree does not just grow taller.

It grows steadier.

REFLECTION

Growth is built the same way furniture is built — piece by piece, tight and honest. A warehouse can become a showroom. Dust can become product. Effort can become opportunity.

I learned that preparation protects you. That showing up prepared saves time, money, and reputation. And I learned that when responsibility increases — when someone is counting on you — your focus sharpens.

Momentum is not magic. It is small things done consistently.

And when a new life is on the way, work stops being ambition. It becomes protection.

GROWTH

1. The Boardroom on Wheels

My business partner and I turned the Brown Camaro into a boardroom at eighty miles an hour because we were calculating the future, not just driving toward it.
Who is sitting in your passenger seat right now, and are they helping you move the venture forward or are they just watching the scenery?

2. The Twice Tax

I told the guard at the DMV that I couldn't afford to come twice because my time was the only currency I had to build a business. Where in your life or business are you paying a "tax" of wasted time because your system isn't tight the first time?

CHAPTER 7

FIRST CUT, FIRST CLAIM (1985–1987)

When the Temperature Changed

When people hear "California dream," they imagine postcards of swaying palm trees, sun-drenched beaches, and the myth of easy money.

My California dream looked different. It showed up as the fine layer of sawdust, a stack of unpaid invoices, a baby's piercing cry at 3:30 a.m., and a business partner who suddenly remembered he liked control more than fairness.

After our first child was born in May 1984, everything shifted.

The warehouse didn't change. It was still the same concrete floor. Containers still arrived and the business was steadily growing. But the partnership changed temperature. The air in the office got cold without anyone opening a window.

My partner sat me down and told me he was cutting my percentage in half. He said I was making too much money and pretty soon I wouldn't need him anymore", he said it with a flat, casual tone, like he was discussing the price of lumber. He talked like I should just accept being reduced at the exact moment I became most responsible.

I swallowed it.

Not because it was right—but because I had a family now. Sometimes you do what you don't want because it's needed at the time.

But something inside me went quiet and clear. I realized then that a partner who takes from you when you need it most isn't a partner at all. He's a lesson. I went back to the warehouse floor, picked up my tools, and kept working.

The roots were holding, but the trunk was being tested. I knew then that the next cut I made wouldn't be for him, it would be for my own claim.

Trust had a crack in it.

And when trust cracks, your body knows before your mind wants to admit it. You start walking carefully, like you're back in those old boots with the hole in the left one. You can still get where you're going, but you feel every single step.

Second Path

I did what I've always done when the ground shifts. I built a second path.

I did it quietly and carefully, with my own hands. I didn't make a speech. I didn't threaten. I didn't try to "win" an argument. I simply planned like a man who knows storms do not ask permission.

I looked at what sold and what customers asked for that we couldn't deliver fast enough. I looked at what would make us different. I started exploring knock-down systems from Italy with better finishes, better lines, and better margins. A wanted a style that didn't look like everybody else's catalog.

I sketched at night when the warehouse was "don't-talk-to-me" quiet. I made calls when the baby finally slept. During the day, I kept my face neutral, like everything was fine.

It was protection, not revenge.

I wasn't trying to take from him. I was trying to make sure no one could take from me again.

The Clean Cut

Six months later, he came to Los Angeles.

He had heard rumors.

He walked into the warehouse with that kind of smile people wear when they've already decided you're guilty. He didn't ask gently. He didn't look for an explanation. He accused.

"You're building your own thing."

I looked at him and felt something odd.

Relief.

Because now the truth was out, and I didn't have to pretend anymore. I told him straight. I didn't apologize for protecting what was mine after he had already taken his cut from my pocket.

Once trust is broken, there is nothing left to hold. It is like a piece of wood with a structural crack. You can sand it, but it will never hold the weight of the house again.

I quit on the spot.

No drama. No screaming. No long story. Just the clean cut.

People think quitting is the brave part. The brave part happens earlier. It is admitting the partnership is already over in your heart, even while you're still showing up and doing the work. It's the quiet decision to stop being a passenger in someone else's vehicle.

That day, I walked out of the warehouse and felt lighter.
I also had something new:
A path that was mine.

Three months before he arrived, I had already rented a shared warehouse and had created my own line. I bought knock down furniture from Italy, using the same system I knew worked. The warehouse was shared, including access to the 24-foot truck and forklift, with only a minimal additional cost. It was exactly what I needed to get started.

Partners

In business, people talk about "partnership" like it's a word on a brochure.

Partnership is not words.
Partnership is behavior.

It's what someone does when you're tired. It's what someone does when you become valuable. It's what someone does when you're feeding a baby and they think you can't afford to fight back.

My partner didn't just cut my commission. He revealed his values. And that was a gift, even if it didn't feel like one at the time.

Some doors close loudly.
This one closed with a quiet sentence:

"Necessary."

After that, I started choosing partners, customers, and employees with one question in mind:

Do they want the job done, or do they want their comfort untouched?

Work for the first.
Keep your vision away from the second.

The Bridge Home

We moved our family from Long Beach to the Pico/Robertson area of Los Angeles. I made the choice because most of my customers were there.

One year later, I found a warehouse that already had everything in place. It came from someone else's setback, but for me, it was the next step forward.

The life I was building required me to be close enough to show up when something broke, when a process slipped, when an employee needed direction. A client's reassurance couldn't wait for a long commute, and the business needed a hand on the wheel at all hours. I was trading a neighborhood for access.

When work grows, everything grows.

The San Fernando Shop

I found a space in San Fernando. It wasn't glamorous. It was a real working shop—a place where the floor had scars and the air had a permanent taste of wood dust and effort.

The machines didn't feel like machines to me. They felt like language I finally knew how to speak. When I turned them on, the sound filled my chest like a drum. It was a reminder that I was back in control.

I hired carpenters who could read my drawings the way musicians read a lead sheet. I didn't write paragraphs. I gave clean measurements, arrows, and sequence. It was the same way I had always worked—efficient, direct, and without noise.

Believe the room, not the drawing.

In the shop, the drawing is just a theory. The room is the reality. If the corner isn't square, the drawing won't fix it. I learned to listen to the space I was in.

I started designing a line that looked like me. I paired natural powder-stone with wood. It had weight. It had presence. It didn't look like cheap furniture pretending to be something else. It looked honest. It was heavy like the crates in the market but refined like the ships in the Navy.

Customers touched it differently. They ran their hands over the surface slower. That's how you know you're onto something. People don't rush when something feels real. They want to linger in the presence of something that wasn't made to be thrown away.

Orders started local.
Then they went wider.
Then they went statewide.
Then they went countrywide.

And at some point, I realized this wasn't just a business. It was translation.

A lot of people wait for motivation.

I didn't just have motivation.
I also had responsibility.

Motivation is a feeling, and feelings change with the weather. Responsibility is an engine. It doesn't care if you're tired. It doesn't care if you fell inspired. It keeps you moving whether you feel like it or not because there are people counting on the output.

Veteran Homeowner

In 1986, we bought our first home on Veteran Street. We lived there for two years. It wasn't fancy; it was functional with an amazing zip code. I looked at that house the same way I looked at a piece of machinery—it was an asset designed to perform a specific task.

Some homes are not dreams; they're bridges. At the time, the Veteran property was not our final destination. It was a steppingstone, a way to keep my family secure while I poured every remaining ounce of energy into the warehouse floor.

The Translation

I had taken everything I learned in Jerusalem—the chaos of the market, the discipline of the bread factory, the vastness of the ship. I had taken the grit of Tel Aviv and the restless hustle of New York and made it all speak California.

It wasn't just a business. It was a synthesis.

For years, I had been collecting parts of a language I didn't know I was learning. The market taught me the value of a quick eye. The factory taught me the necessity of a system. The ship taught me how to respect the weight of things.

In California, I finally put them all together. I wasn't just building furniture. I was building a bridge between where I had been and where I was determined to go.

I stopped being a student of the struggle. I became a master of the work.

TREE WISDOM

A tree stops being a seedling the moment it holds its ground. Growth isn't always about adding. Sometimes, it is about the cut.

A broken branch doesn't mean the tree is failing; it means the tree is redirecting its sap.

The cut is ugly. It hurts. But after the cut, the tree is forced to be honest about where its real strength lies.

REFLECTION

I didn't leave the partnership, the partnership left me by breaking trust. I learned that fairness is never guaranteed, but integrity is a choice you make every day.

A quiet exit is almost always stronger than a loud argument. Building my own path wasn't an act of arrogance—it was an act of responsibility. I stopped waiting for someone to give me a seat at the table and decided to build the table myself.

GROWTH

1. The Expensive Boundary

Trust often changes long before the words are spoken.
Where has trust changed in your life—and what boundary are you avoiding because confrontation feels too expensive?

2. The Second Path

I planned quietly and carefully so that the storm wouldn't catch me without a roof.

What "second path" can you build right now—a skill, a savings account, or a network—that protects your future?

3. The Strength of the Cut

A broken branch isn't a failure. It is a redirection of strength to where it is needed most.

What part of your life needs a "clean cut" today so that you can finally be honest about where your real strength lies?

CHAPTER 8

WHEN BRANCHES BEGIN TO SPREAD (1987–1992)

The Wind Gets Stronger

When branches spread, you feel the wind more. Success didn't arrive for me as applause. It arrived as a heavier kind of responsibility.

By the late eighties, the shop in San Fernando was no longer fragile. Orders came in steadily. Designers started calling instead of me chasing them. Contractors asked for repeat installs. The line of furniture had an identity now. It wasn't borrowed. It wasn't copied. It was ours. It felt like the ground under my feet was finally solid, but that solidity came with a new kind of gravity.

With that growth came something I hadn't felt before: Exposure.

When I was small, I was invisible. As I grew, people started measuring me. They measured my word, my deadlines, and the way I handled the inevitable mistake.

Payroll Has Weight

I hired more carpenters. Then installers. Then office support. Payroll became a weekly reality, not a future hope. A mistake wasn't just my mistake anymore. It was a ripple that hit everyone. It affected families. It affected mortgages. It affected children's school lunches.

That changes how you sleep.

At first, growth feels like expansion—more orders, more trucks, a bigger space. But what I realized I was actually expanding weight. Every new branch pulled on the trunk. Every new employee pulled on the system. I saw then that if the trunk isn't thick enough, the tree will snap under the weight of its own success. I wasn't just building furniture for customers anymore.

I was building a shelter for other people's lives.

The Limit of Instinct

That's when something became clear: Skill builds a business, but structure sustains it.

Up until then, my advantage was instinct.

I could read a room. I could read a customer. I could solve on the fly. But instinct does not scale. When you have twenty deliveries in one week across three counties, instinct becomes chaos. You cannot "vibe" your way through a supply chain.

I began building systems the same way I built shelves.
Piece by piece.

I looked at every bottleneck and realized that a good system is just a series of honest decisions that you've automated so you don't have to be in ten places at once.

We moved to clear drawings, clear measurements, and clear delivery schedules. No guessing.

We created checklists before leaving the warehouse. Hardware bags labeled twice. Tools counted before and after jobs. Install photos documented. Payment terms written cleanly.

I saw the shift in the shop immediately. Some employees loved the clarity.
Some didn't.

Discipline is attractive until it becomes required. I lost a few good workers because they preferred freedom without conditions. I understood that—I used to be that way, too.

The work needed to function even when I wasn't standing in the room.

The Other Branch: Home

At home, the branches were growing, too. But I wasn't always there to see it happen.

The business was growing in numbers. The home was growing in noise. Both were asking for a version of me that didn't get tired, but the shop usually won the coin toss.

My wife and I were no longer just surviving in a basement; we were building a household. She built the homefront foundation while I built the furniture to fill it. Diapers became school forms. Night feedings became early soccer practices. I would come home from the shop covered in sawdust, and my daughter would run toward me without caring how much money we made that week.

Children don't measure revenue.
They measure presence.
And my presence was spread thin.

That was the season I noticed a quieter, harder reality:
You cannot grow every branch at once.

In the shop, I knew how to prune a tree to make it grow straight. I knew that if you let every branch grow wild, the center eventually weakens. I was reaching for more market share and more production convinced that "providing" was the same thing as "being there."
I was building a forest, but I was missing the growth of my own trees.

I had to learn how to be "all there" when I walked through the front door, even if the sawdust was still in my hair and the problems of the shop were still shouting in my head.

The Temptation of Growth

I had opportunities to expand faster. There were bigger warehouses, second locations, and investors who liked the margins and wanted to pour fuel on the fire. It was the kind of temptation that wears a suit and shakes your hand confidently.

But I remembered the market days. I knew that if the structure leans, everything pays for it later.

I chose steady over spectacular.

We reinvested carefully. We paid down debt before we upgraded equipment. I focused on increasing our margins before we increased our footprint. It wasn't flashy, but it was sustainable. I didn't want a "hot" company; I wanted a solid one that would still be standing when the trend shifted.

Choosing Value Over Price

In those years, competition grew. Cheap imports started flooding the market—knock-offs, lower prices, and faster production. Customers who once valued the weight of real wood began asking for discounts, comparing my hand-built units to something made in a factory half a world away.

I could feel the pressure shifting again.

This time the pressure wasn't personal. It was the market. It was an economic wind that didn't care about my history or my long hours. I stood in the warehouse one afternoon, looking at a display unit we had built with real wood and real weight, and I had to decide.

Do we compete on price or on value?

I watched others choose price. It looked like a race to the bottom, where someone was always willing to go a dollar lower until no one can make a living. Competing on value is a longer road, but it actually leads somewhere.

I decided to take the longer road.

We focused on the value—better finishes, better installation guarantees and cleaner showrooms. We made mistakes, we corrected them publicly and refused to hide the flaws.

That built reputation. And reputation doesn't shout.
It accumulates.

Holding up the Bridge

By this time, I was a business owner with employees, contracts, and a mountain of responsibility.

And still, most mornings, I felt like a bridge carrying more weight than it was designed for.

Growth doesn't erase insecurity.
It just gives it a larger stage.

Growth can bring large orders that are delayed, checks that bounce, and orders that get canceled for one reason or another. I understood it was part of doing business. It came with the territory. In those moments, I had to quiet the chaos in my head and return to the same words that sustained me from the beginning:

Start.
Keep going.
You will arrive.

Progress is sometimes dramatic, but it's simply refusing to stop. Those words never promised me speed. They promised direction. When the bridge is rickety, I didn't sprint. I took one step at a time. One foot after the other until I reached the other side.

Looking back, that era was not about expansion. It was about restraint.

I realized that the health of the tree wasn't measured by how wide my branches spread, but by whether my trunk could carry them without splitting. It was the season I stopped trying to prove myself to the world and started protecting what I built.

TREE WISDOM

A tree that spreads its branches without thickening its trunk is just waiting for the wind to break it. Growth is a trap if it isn't supported by structure.

Trees don't just grow "out"—they have to grow "strong." Every new leaf requires a new level of support from the roots.

REFLECTION

Growth tested my ego and my patience. I learned that expansion without structure is just decoration. I learned that value outlasts discounts. And I learned that not every opportunity deserves a yes.

Most importantly, I learned that presence at home matters more than applause outside.

GROWTH

1. The Weight of Exposure

When you are small, you are invisible, but success brings you into the open.

Is your character strong enough to be measured by others?

How have you prepared for the "wind" that comes with being seen?

2. The Instinct Wall

I realized that my gut feelings couldn't handle the weight of a scaling business at that moment.
Where in your life or business is your "instinct" telling you something you should listen to?

3. The Payroll Sleep

The realization that the system's mistakes affected other people's lives changed the way I viewed my work.
Who is currently relying on the strength of your "trunk," and how are you ensuring you don't snap under the weight?

CHAPTER 9

THE WIND CHANGES DIRECTION (1986–1995)

The Markets Starts Whispering

There is a moment in every long season when the air feels different before anything looks different. The phones still ring. The shop still runs. Customers still want delivery dates. But underneath it, the market shifts its weight, and I felt it in my margins long before I saw it on paper.

For me, that shift came quietly through imported furniture. The cheaper it got, the more I could see the future tightening around my business like a belt pulled one notch at a time. I loved the craft. I loved walking into a furniture showroom and leaving it better than I found it.

But love is not a business plan.

I wasn't just competing with the shop down the street—I was competing with global logistics and mass production. If I stayed where I was, I would eventually be squeezed out by a price tag I couldn't match.

Over time I built a name, then momentum, and eventually capacity, until the business needed a larger body to match its appetite.

Within two years I moved us into a much bigger factory in South Gate near Downtown Los Angeles. It was a massive, echoing space that felt both like a victory and a gamble. We expanded production, attended international shows, and opened markets I never could have reached. Manufacturing gives you authority in your own life.

The Strategy of Ownership

A couple of years later, we took another leap. We rented out the first house on Veteran, and we upgraded again to a larger home on Redwood Avenue. It was a better neighborhood with better schools and more space. We would end up living there for fifteen years—long enough for the house to become part of our DNA.

It felt like the kind of home where routines would finally settle, and the walls would memorize the specific frequency of our children's voices and the rhythm of their footsteps. It was where stability stopped being an idea and started becoming structure. Looking back, it was one of those rare moments where patience and planning finally shook hands.

Children change what walls mean. To a builder, they are square footage and studs. To a parent, they are safety. They are continuity. They are the boundary between the world's noise and your family's peace.

The walls around finally me belonged to us.

Stability Has a Smell

Stability has a smell—fresh paint and cardboard boxes.

The house came first. The real estate investments came after. I knew that stability for the family had to be a concrete reality before I could afford to take bigger risks. I needed a floor that wouldn't give way.

While my hands were still calloused from building furniture, my eyes were already shifting. It wasn't that I wanted to abandon the craft. I just needed a contingency plan. I could feel the furniture market being squeezed, the margins getting thinner with every factory-made piece that hit the showrooms.

I had spent years watching handcrafted tables and chairs lose value. I was tired of chasing a depreciating asset. I wanted to own something that gained value while I slept.

I didn't announce my move. I didn't dramatize the shift. I did what I've always done when I could feel weather coming.

I started studying the room.

Learning the Neighborhoods

For years, I entered other people's homes carrying tools. At first, I saw rooms as assignments. Install the wardrobe. Level the shelves. Fix the hinge. Collect the check.

But over time, something shifted. I began noticing ceiling height, the specific way the light hit the living room in the late afternoon, the angles of the walls, the flow from the kitchen to the dining area. I wasn't just looking at the furniture anymore—I was looking at the skeleton of the house.

I started noticing the street noise, the parking, the proximity of the schools, and the invisible difference between a block that holds value and a block that leaks it.

Customers talked about storage. I was thinking about layout, land, and leverage.

I started reading the street the way I used to read a soccer field. I looked for which houses had people sitting outside at dusk. Which blocks felt watched over. Which corners were loud for no reason. Where kids rode bikes without fear.

In Jerusalem, I learned that a street has a heartbeat. You can tell who is moving in and who is giving up just by looking at the paint on the doors. In L.A., I realized that neighborhoods have the same pulse. I wasn't looking for the most expensive house—I was looking for the one that was "holding its breath"—the house that was better than its condition, waiting for someone with a level and a saw to wake it up.

A cracked tile stopped looking like damage. It started looking like negotiating room. An outdated kitchen stopped looking sad. It started looking underpriced relative to the effort needed to improve it.

Most investors see a "fixer-upper" as a headache they have to pay someone else to solve. I saw it as a profit margin I could manufacture with my own two hands. My tools weren't just for making furniture anymore—they were for unlocking equity.

If I know how to increase value inside a home, why am I not buying the home first?

That question stayed with me.

The First Leap: Venice Triplex (1989)

In 1989, I didn't have a portfolio or a private banker. I had built a system that worked from sawdust and sweat, and a vision for a triplex on Victoria Avenue in Venice.

Signing those papers felt like a victory lap. I remember walking out of that office feeling the pull of both sides at once. The excitement of the opportunity, and the weight that came with it. Tenants already living there. Repairs waiting in the dark. Units I would have to fill when they were empty.

I was trying to get stable permanently. I realized that business can be taken from you by unfair competition or a bad partner, but a deed is a different kind of anchor. I wanted to build a wall of assets so thick that my children would never even have to know what a basement window felt like.

I didn't have "investor capital." I had hustle, a high tolerance for risk, and the stubborn belief that I could make the math work. Most importantly, I had a skill most people didn't respect until they were in trouble: I wasn't afraid of fixing things.

Renovation didn't scare me. It felt natural, like breathing.

I became a student of the trade. I watched the hired handymen, the electricians, the plumbers, the painters, and the tile workers. I didn't just pay them. I interrogated them. I watched, I asked, I practiced, and I got better. Most investors see a leaking pipe as a crisis they have to pay to disappear. I saw it as a classroom. Every time I patched a wall or fixed a sink myself, I was lowering my overhead and manufacturing my own equity with my own two hands.

Tight, not fast. Structure before speed.

That was the rule that traveled with me from bread crates to baseboards.

The triplex worked. It wasn't just a deal. It was proof. Proof that a building could keep paying even when a market got noisy. Proof that I could secure revenue without being trapped in the gravity of a single industry.

When the Family Grows

Life wasn't only business during those years. Our family expanded too. Two more beautiful daughters were born in 1990 and 1992, and suddenly, the hallways of our home had a new rhythm.

A house full of daughters changes a man's definition of success. The weight of my "why" grew with every new voice in the house.

When children arrive, a house becomes louder, fuller, tighter in the best possible way. It's proof that building something solid under your family changes the way you sleep at night.

Children are the best investment, but they are also the most expensive. And I'm not talking about the cost of diapers, food, or school.
They cost responsibility.

When your family grows, you stop thinking only about what you can build. You start thinking about what you can protect. Before children, risk feels exciting—a shot of adrenaline. After children, risk feels a little heavy. The decisions remain the same, but the gravity pulling on them is different.

By then, I was still running the furniture business—still designing, still producing, and still holding my ground while cheap imports began to flood the market and change the rules of the game. Real estate wasn't replacing furniture.

It was becoming the foundation underneath it.
The fourth leg of the table.

Scaling Up: The Partner and the Bigger Leap

Not long after, I met a man who wanted to partner with me on a bigger real estate play: two apartment buildings, twenty-four units each.

Forty-eight apartments total.

In my mind, these weren't just forty-eight "units." They were forty-eight families. Forty-eight plus toilets that could break at 2:00 a.m. Forty-eight stories I was now responsible for, whether I felt like it or not.

In the Bronx, I learned to carry one carton at a time. In Venice, I learned to carry one building. But forty-eight units isn't just more weight—it's a different kind of gravity. You stop being the guy with the tools, and you start being the guy with the plan.

That's where I learned the difference between being handy and being structured. Handiness saves a day. Structure saves a decade.

This was a different world than a triplex. The conversations got heavier. The paperwork grew thicker. Banks. Terms. Guarantees. Tenant management. Maintenance realities. Expense ratios. Cash flow buffers.

I had to learn to build something I could trust, not just rely on my own muscle.
If the structure is weak, the muscle doesn't matter.

It wasn't scary. It just demanded a different kind of discipline—one built in, not forced.

We did it. We rented the units.
And with that, something simple and invaluable became clear:

Be open to listen and learn from experienced businesspeople. It always serves.

With that partner, I learned how to buy larger buildings and units, how to navigate banks without getting swallowed by them, and how to manage the invisible chaos that leaks money when you aren't paying attention.

Furniture taught me this: mistakes show up immediately. Real estate taught me something new: mistakes can hide until conditions change.

In a shop, if a cut is crooked, you see it before the glue dries. You feel the wobble in the chair the moment you set it down. But in real estate, a bad "cut" in the paperwork or a flaw in the math might stay hidden for years. It lies dormant in the walls of the deal, only showing up when the market turns cold and the heat goes out. I had to learn to look for the rot before the storm hit.

I learned to respect the numbers the way I respected a level, not as a suggestion, but as a requirement. If the bubble isn't centered, the shelf is wrong. If the math isn't centered, the future is crooked.

Real estate, like life, does not move in straight lines. Permits stall. Costs rise. Plans change. There were moments standing on construction sites where the numbers did not quite add up and the future felt uncertain. Those were the moments that tested whether the lessons from earlier years—work, patience, responsibility—were truly part of who I had become.

The grit isn't in the building; it's in staying steady when the building is delayed.

The Hidden Structure

Buildings rise slowly.
Character rises the same way.

Like roots growing underground, most of the real work happens before anyone sees the structure break the surface. People see the factory in South Gate or the apartment buildings in Venice and they call it "success." They don't see the years I spent carrying crates in the sun or the quiet nights I spent learning the language of a typewriter. They see the branches. They don't see the roots. But without the roots, the building doesn't stand a chance.

Success is a high-rise, but struggle is the basement that keeps it from falling. If you don't spend time in the dirt, you won't know how to stand in the sun.

I realized that every "no" I had to swallow and every "clean cut" I had to make in my life was just digging the foundation deeper. By the mid-nineties, the structure of my life was finally starting to show above the dirt. It wasn't just a shop or a house. It was a character that had been built to hold weight.

The Shift in the Wind

After a couple of years, I began to feel something I've learned to trust: the sense that the wind is shifting again.

My partner and I wanted different things. I could feel him slowing down. I could also feel him pulling me deeper into the operational problems—maintenance issues, tenant friction, constant repairs—because that's where my skills made the system run better.

And I understood it. Those things mattered.

But in business, you can't spend your life fixing the same leaks if you want to sail to a new ocean. My skills were in my hands, but my vision was in my head. I had to choose which one to follow.

The Second Foundation

By the mid-nineties, the second foundation was no longer an idea. It was active.

I knew what I wanted: to acquire more properties, build a team, and scale without turning my life into an endless maintenance call. I needed employees to handle the tasks so I could handle the vision. I wanted my role to be direction, acquisition, standards, and strategy.

I didn't do the dramatic thing. I did the clean thing.

I told him we should split. We settled our affairs and separated our paths with the kind of quiet respect that only comes after you've bled and built together. I didn't feel anger. I felt clarity. Sometimes relationships don't end because something went wrong. They end because the direction of the path has changed.

Some partnerships end in a flurry of arguments and broken trust. Ours ended with a quiet understanding. We had built something solid, but the wind had shifted, and our roads were no longer parallel. The growth was elsewhere now, and I had to move with it.

That shift marked the beginning of the next chapter.

TREE WISDOM

A tree that has grown too large for its original plot doesn't need more water; it needs a wider field.

My roots had reached the edge of the partnership. Separation wasn't an act of betrayal; it was an act of survival.

If you don't recognize when your growth has outpaced your surroundings, you eventually start to rot in place.

REFLECTION

I learned that the hardest part of scaling up is letting go of the tasks you're good at so you can focus on the tasks you're needed for. I was a great handyman, but that was no longer my job. I realized that a "clean exit" is the ultimate professional skill. You don't need a bridge to burn to know it's time to cross it.

GROWTH

1. The Market Whisper

I felt the shift in my business long before it showed up on a balance sheet. Intuition is just experience whispering in your ear.

Is the "wind" in your current situation—at school, in a relationship, or at work—changing?

Are you listening to the quiet whisper of your gut or waiting for the scream of a crisis to make a move?

2. The Task Trap

Being "handy" was enough to manage a handful of units, but managing forty-eight required a "system" that didn't need my physical presence. I had to leave a partnership because I was "too good" at maintenance. My skill was becoming my cage, keeping me from my vision.

Where in your life are you exhausting yourself by trying to "handyman" everything (doing it all yourself)?

What is one thing you can turn into a "system" or a routine so it can survive and grow without you hovering over it?

CHAPTER 10

WHEN GROWTH SPLITS A TREE IN TWO (1995-2009)

L.A. Apartments Biz Seed

Bargaining your days for pennies ensures you will always miss the dollars. By 1995, that realization had become my operational base.

In the beginning, the "company" was a secretary, and two maintenance employees, a phone, a desk, and a stack of folders.

But every enduring entity begins like that: not with a polished logo, but with the raw weight of responsibility.

I launched L.A. Apartments Biz with a slogan that was as much a personal standard as it was a brand:
"We do better :)"

To me, "better" wasn't surface-level. It was the standard behind everything. It meant providing dignity—for tenants, for employees, and for the families living inside the walls I now owned.

Two Businesses, One Nervous System

For three years, I lived in the friction between two entirely different worlds. Day and night, I was navigating the sawdust and precision of the furniture factory and managing the system and logistics of tenant needs and property acquisitions. It felt like maintaining two separate trunks on a single root system. I could feel the tension in the wood—the specific strain that happens right before a tree is forced to choose a direction.

As the real estate portfolio grew, I brought in a trusted friend to help manage the moving parts. This wasn't about handing over the vision. It was about buying breathing room. I needed to ensure I could keep reaching without letting the standard slip.

The furniture business had built me, but I felt its season was coming to an end. My exit wasn't going to be about losing passion for the craft; it was an acknowledgement that the terrain had changed. I had more at stake now—people and properties that required a different, more present version of me.

That smile in the slogan wasn't added for decoration. It was a promise that standards would not drop just because the portfolio grew. It was a reminder that buildings are not just assets—they are homes. People living inside your walls should feel the difference between an owner who is present and one who treats them like a line on a spreadsheet.

The truth is, transitions are rarely clean. In real life, you don't always get to close one door before opening another. Sometimes, you hold two heavy doors open at once, even when your hands are already tired.

The House on Redwood Avenue

Those were high-velocity years, the kind where dinner is a backdrop for a contractor's call and bedtime stories are sidelined by a tenant's emergency. My mind was a split-screen, constantly running a second track in the background even while I tried to be present in the living room.

In the quiet gaps, I found moments of ordinary beauty that didn't care about my business ambitions. It was the scent of Persian rice steam filling the room and the obstacle course of toys left in the hallway.

The house on Redwood Avenue was a symphony of small chaos: children's laughter, the rhythmic thud of feet on the floor, the constant hum of a young family.

The End of the Furniture Era

By 2003, the pressure on the furniture business became a physical weight. The U.S. markets had opened wide to China, and a flood of cheap, mass-produced pieces hit our shores with the force of a tidal wave. Suddenly, customers who once valued custom design and the soul of craftsmanship began comparing numbers first. When a market trains people to value price above all else, it changes the entire vocabulary of your industry.

I watched the orders thin out. In a move that still makes me shake my head, I tried to pivot toward importing cheaper furniture from China. It was a compromise born of survival—a decision that my pride hated but my bank account demanded. But trying to compete on those terms was like racing a machine that never gets tired. There is no way to out-hustle a factory that doesn't value the individual.

By 2004, the math had turned cold. It made no sense—and no profit—to keep the doors open. My passion was in the design, the tactile reality of the wood, and closing that factory hurt in a way that wasn't just financial. That building held decades of my identity. Closing it felt like cutting down a tree I had raised from a seed—one that had fed my family and sheltered my confidence for years.

But I wasn't standing in an empty field. I had a backup. And that backup was about to become my life's work.

Betrayal and the Cost of Trust

Then I learned the kind of lesson you never want to learn. It started with the small details that didn't fit—a receipt that didn't match, materials disappearing faster than the schedule allowed, or a worker casually mentioning a job I hadn't approved. My stomach knew the truth long before my brain finished the math.

I thought I understood distrust, but this was a different animal. I discovered that the friend that I brought on to lighten my load was using my materials and my employees to renovate his own projects on the side, essentially feeding his business with the resources I had painstakingly built.

When the truth finally surfaced, I bought him out and ended it immediately. Betrayal from a stranger hits your wallet, but betrayal from someone close hits your nervous system. It makes you question your own instincts and forces you to rebuild not just your business controls, but your internal sense of trust.

Some people lie to you, then they lie to themselves by believing in the lie, and finally, they have the audacity to act offended when you call it what it is. That experience pushed me into a deeper level of structure. I tightened operations and built rigorous systems, increasing oversight not out of a desire to be suspicious, but because I finally understood that scale without controls isn't freedom—it's vulnerability.

Dignity Lives In the Details

As I became more involved in the day-to-day operations, I saw a massive opening in the market that others were ignoring. So many apartment buildings across Los Angeles and the San Fernando Valley were neglected and undervalued simply because the work was unglamorous. The neighborhoods weren't trendy and the buildings were tired, owned by people who didn't want to deal with the daily realities of tenants and repairs.

That became my lane. I wasn't afraid of the hard work, and I certainly wasn't afraid of "unwanted" areas if the math was sound and the need was real. People will always need housing, and simple, well-managed living spaces will always matter.

I focused my energy on renovating the buildings where others hesitated, learning along the way that improving a property isn't just about fresh paint and new plumbing. True improvement is found in management, consistency, and the quiet sense that someone is actually watching the details.

The 2008 Crash

Momentum can be a dangerous drug. I was moving aggressively, expanding with the market, until 2008 arrived and the country learned what systemic fear looked like.

Homes were lost, credit lines froze, and a wave of panic leveled the industry. It was a somber, heavy season—not a time for celebration, but a time to be absolutely steady. While I took a hit alongside everyone else, I was able to keep covering expenses because I had refused to overleverage myself. My intuition told me something that felt risky but sounded right: while the rest of the world was paralyzed by fear, this was the moment to double down with precision.

The hard truth of that year was that opportunity and tragedy often sit at the same table. I realized then that a person can move strategically without enjoying anyone else's pain; compassion doesn't have to be the enemy of a sound business decision.

When the House Grows Quiet

Business success has a way of masking personal erosion. As the company stabilized and grew, the external noise of my life—the deals, the contractors, the expansion—finally began to drown out the internal frequency of my home. I was so focused on building the fortress that I didn't notice the life inside it was growing quieter.

As the company expanded, so did the distance within our walls. Our youngest daughter was preparing to leave for college, and while my wife could feel the house changing, I was still looking toward the next horizon. She saw the quiet that was coming; I saw only the next opportunity. Where she imagined empty rooms, I imagined new acquisitions.

With the house empty and the daily "symphony of small chaos" gone, the silence between me and my wife became impossible to ignore. We had spent so many years focusing on the logistics of the family that we hadn't noticed we were growing apart.

It's a painful irony: you sacrifice your presence to build a foundation for the people you love, only to find that the very act of building has pulled you away from the life you were trying to protect. By the time I looked up from the blueprints, the distance had become a canyon. I had to face the reality that some things, once broken by neglect, cannot be renovated.

I stopped trying to force the past into a shape it no longer fit. Letting go of those familiar rhythms and the old version of myself as the "provider" who was never home was a difficult pruning. But that space was necessary. I had to make room for the man I needed to become for the season ahead: one who finally understood that a legacy isn't what you leave for people, but what you leave in them.

TREE WISDOM

Success adds weight faster than roots can grow.

Sometimes the branch you remove is not dead; it's simply pulling the trunk in the wrong direction. You prune it not out of anger, but for survival.

REFLECTION

Starting L.A. Apartments Biz was a declaration that my next season would be built on structure, not improvisation. The stakes had changed. When the furniture market collapsed under global competition, I saw that passion requires protection—and that protection comes from building a second foundation before the first one cracks. When trust broke with someone close, it became clear that leadership isn't just about vision; it is about the systems that prevent that vision from being compromised.

GROWTH

1. The Pruning of the Living

Most people only change when they are forced to by failure. I chose to move while the furniture factory was still active. True growth requires the discipline to look past today's "busy-ness" to see where the market is actually heading. It's about having the courage to leave a familiar path before it turns into a dead end. What is currently working in your life that you know, deep down, is not part of your long-term future? How do you begin the transition before the "choice" is taken away from you?

2. The Second Foundation

I didn't wait for the furniture factory to close before I started L.A. Apartments Biz. I built a bridge while I was still standing on the old one. If I had waited for the first foundation to crumble entirely, I wouldn't have had the strength to start again.

Do you have a "second foundation" in development, or are you waiting for your current season to end before looking for the next one?

3. The Empty Fortress

Building a business, a hobby, or even a digital reputation can mask the erosion of what's real. I realized too late that a foundation built for the family is useless if the builder is rarely inside the house. Whether you are building an empire or a social life, the danger is the same: you can become so focused on the outside image that you neglect the inner reality.

In your pursuit of "providing" or "fitting in," are you accidentally neglecting the people who actually know you?

What is one "blueprint" in your personal life—a relationship, a habit, or a home dynamic—that needs an immediate, hands-on renovation?

4. The Power of the Slogan

When I started L.A. Apartments Biz, I didn't just pick a name; I picked a mission: **"We do better :)"** It was a simple promise that kept me accountable when things got challenging. A slogan might be how you decide to treat people or how you handle a setback. It could be a standard you refuse to drop when the market gets crowded. A slogan is an internal compass that tells you which way to turn when you're lost.

If you were to name your next life chapter, what would your slogan be?

CHAPTER 11

SUCCESS AND SILENCE (2009-Present)

The Empty Feeling

I was standing in the kitchen with the lights off, eating something straight from the fridge like a teenager. The house was large enough to echo, a sprawling proof of everything I had built. From the outside, my life looked full—perfect even. But standing there in the dark, the silence was overwhelming.

It wasn't depression, exactly—it was an absence. It was as if the volume of my life had been turned up to the maximum, but the meaning had been set to mute. Something essential was thinning out. It is a difficult truth to admit, but my greatest success had become my quietest failure. In the early years, when my daughters were small and the business demanded every ounce of my energy, I convinced myself there would be more time later.

Later finally came, but it looked nothing like I had imagined

When the Tree Splits Again

By 2013, the distance between us was no longer something we could bridge with effort or intention. Thirty years is a long time to share a life with someone. It is long enough for habits to become a private language, for silence to become understood, and for conflict to become a routine. When we finally hugged and cried, it wasn't out of anger; it was the heavy acknowledgment that this ending had become inevitable.

When I folded my clothes into a single suitcase and walked out the door, I wasn't just leaving a marriage. I was walking away from the version of myself I had spent three decades trying to protect.

I checked into a hotel close by and told myself it would be temporary, the way businessmen tell themselves most things are temporary.

A negotiation. A cooling-off period.

Something that could be stabilized if managed correctly. That had always been my instinct, stabilize, leverage, fix. But there are seasons in life that do not respond to management. Both of us understood that. What I really needed was to face what I had been avoiding for years.

The Ocean and the Quiet

After a month of hotel rooms and room service trays stacked outside the door, I rented an apartment overlooking the Santa

Monica beach. From the balcony, the Pacific stretched out wide and indifferent. The tide moved in and out with the same rhythm every day, unconcerned with the strange quiet that now followed me from room to room.

I had built something enormous in the world. Thousands of living spaces. Hundreds of employees. Properties that had multiplied over decades through discipline and risk and intuition. Banks returned my calls. Deals closed. My name carried weight.

And yet in that apartment, with the sound of waves rising through the open windows at night, I understood something uncomfortable: I did not know how to be still.

My entire life had been defined by motion—expansion, acquisition, improvement, and growth. In the silence of the beach, that stillness felt like exposure. It felt like standing without armor. I began to see that my ambition, which I had always celebrated as a strength, had also served as a shield. As long as I was building, I didn't have to face what was buried underneath the noise.

Running From the Quiet

When a friend in Israel invited me to visit and "take a break," the "yes" was out of my mouth before he could finish the sentence. I told myself I needed distance—a change of air, a reminder of where I came from. But in truth, I was simply trying to outrun the silence of that apartment in Santa Monica.

I stayed at the Dan Hotel in Tel Aviv. Once again, I chose a room facing the water, as if staring at the horizon could somehow widen the space inside me. My days became a blur of restaurants and crowded tables, filled with the kind of laughter that sounds convincing from the outside. In the middle of that noise, I met someone. She was warm, intelligent and attentive. She felt like possibility.

At that time, I was not looking for depth. I was looking for relief. There is a vital difference between the two.

When loneliness presses against your ribs long enough, new companionship can feel like oxygen. I convinced myself timing was right, that this was the natural beginning of a new chapter. Friends cautioned me. They had seen my exhaustion. They suggested I slow down. But I had never built my life by slowing down.

I moved forward.

The Pattern

Six years later, when that relationship unraveled, I was forced to face the recurring math of my life. The scenery had changed—the apartment was different, the city had shifted—but the underlying restlessness remained untouched. I had spent six years adding new branches to a tree without ever checking the health of the soil.

Digging Up Roots

I began therapy during that season, not as a desperate attempt to repair a marriage, but as a necessary excavation of myself. What I discovered in those sessions wasn't elegant. It wasn't the kind of "inspirational" breakthrough you see in movies. It was raw, jagged, and uncomfortable.

For decades, I had functioned at a high level while carrying a massive, unexamined weight. I had locked away childhood experiences because there was simply no room for vulnerability in the environments where I was raised. I suppressed the frustration of a dyslexia that made classrooms feel like hostile territory and the confusion of being a left-handed child in a time when that difference was treated as a defect to be corrected rather than a trait to be understood. I carried family trauma that was only ever spoken of in whispers—or not at all.

In my world, strength had always meant endurance. But in that room, I discovered that endurance was no longer enough.
The hardest part wasn't the talking; it was the stillness. It was sitting long enough to finally notice everything I had been running from my entire life. Those first sessions felt like a vault I had welded shut was being forced open against its will. The pressure built in my chest and my head simultaneously, followed by the unfamiliar, unbidden sensation of tears coming without permission.

As a child, I had been told that men do not cry. I had learned that lesson too well. But grief doesn't disappear just because you deny it. It simply accumulates, influencing the speed at which you work, the tone of your voice, and the razor-thin tolerance you have for imperfection—in others, and especially in yourself.

I had mastered leverage in the business world, but I was a novice at the leverage of emotion. My empire had grown outward much faster than my roots had grown inward.

Better late, than never.

Start.
Keep going.
You will arrive.

And when you do,
you'll realize you were never lost.
Just still growing roots.

TREE WISDOM

The tallest trees grow in silence.
They are not chasing the sky.
They are answering the soil.

A tree can survive strong winds only if its roots grow as deeply as its branches rise. Success without self-knowledge creates height without stability.

REFLECTION

For decades, I mistook endurance for strength. I thought that pushing through pain, solving external problems, and expanding my capacity were the only metrics that mattered. But real strength includes the courage to be soft. It includes the willingness to look at old wounds instead of burying them under a mountain of productivity. The experiences I once tried to outrun were never obstacles—they were the shaping forces of my life. I just had to be still enough to see them.

The wind was never the enemy. Avoiding the roots was.

GROWTH

1. The Cost of Responsibility

We often use "being responsible" or "being busy" as a socially acceptable way to hide from our feelings. We postpone grief, fear, or joy because we have "work to do." But unaddressed emotions don't disappear; they just wait for the wind to blow hard enough to expose them. What emotions or truths have you postponed because you were "too busy" or "too responsible" to feel them?

2. The Illusion of Height

It is easy to measure your life by how high you've climbed—your grades, your bank account, social status, or your career title. But if you grow upward without growing inward, you are just building a taller tower on a shallow foundation. Where in your life have you grown upward without growing inward?

3. The Living Headline

Most people spend their lives writing a thousand pages, but in the end, the world only remembers a single sentence. That sentence is your legacy. It's not about the money you made or the buildings you raised; it's about the core frequency of your character.

If your legacy had one sentence, what would you want your children (or team) to say you stood for?

EPILOGUE

THE ROOTS REVOLUTION

When I look back now, I don't see buildings first. I see seasons.

I see the boy who struggled in school because the letters moved differently for him. I see the young man who left home with more determination than clarity. I see the husband who mistook providing for being present, and the businessman who convinced himself that expansion was the only form of protection.

Each season felt permanent while I was inside it. It never is.

Veteran Street in 1986 felt like arrival. Redwood Avenue in 1988 felt like security. The Venice triplex in 1989 felt like strategy. The factory closures felt like loss. The real estate crash felt like risk. The divorce felt like failure. Therapy felt like exposure.

None of them turned out to be final.

Trees do not grow in straight lines. They thicken where storms hit hardest, and the rings you cannot see often tell the real story.

For many years, I leaned into leverage as the primary key to growth. Financially, it was. But leverage without awareness eventually becomes pressure, and pressure without reflection eventually becomes fracture.

I have lived long enough now to understand something I could not see in my thirties or forties: success is not measured by scale alone. For me, it has become about integration.

Today the business runs with hundreds of employees, thousands of living spaces, and systems in motion. It no longer depends on my constant grip. I worked hard to build something durable, but what matters more to me now is building something deeper.

For many years I believed I had to hold everything up myself. That belief helped me build, but it also cost me closeness, time, and softness. These days I find myself thinking less about how much I can carry and more about how open I can remain.

Looking back, if there is anything I would quietly pass on to the next generation, whether they are building their lives, their families, their businesses, or all of them at once, it is simply this: growing tall means very little if the roots underneath are thin.

Next Chapters — Love and Legacy

For most of my life, my focus was on building structures outside of me. I measured my progress in square footage, acquisitions, and the physical security of a growing empire. But as the seasons shift,

I find myself learning a different kind of architecture—the kind that is built from within.

For a long time, I believed I understood love. Looking back, what I really understood was loyalty, responsibility, and the deep-seated instinct to provide.

Those are essential, but love turns out to be more than just "staying." It asks for presence without armor and strength without the need for control. I am still learning that. Perhaps that is the most honest thing I can say about it today.

The next chapters of my life are more about alignment. I have come to see that success without love feels hollow, while love without responsibility rarely holds. The real work is learning how to hold to both.

Trees do not erase their scars. They grow around them. A knot in the trunk is not a flaw; it is a record of a season survived. The scar becomes part of the tree's unique strength.

I am no longer interested in polishing over the broken parts of my life. I am far more interested in learning through them and growing from them.

The path ahead isn't about building more.
It's about building deeper.
It's about becoming a man my daughters and grandchildren can learn from and grow close to, not just benefit from monetarily.

Deep roots do not grow overnight. They grow through daily choices. Through those choices, I continue learning how to do better.

Storms are part of the design. The goal is not to avoid them, but to grow deep enough that the wind does not decide who you are. The wind, I've learned, is not the enemy. Shallow roots are.

Strength and success were never meant to stop with one person. What we hold too tightly eventually shrinks, but what we share has a way of growing beyond us.

We are not separate stories competing for space; we are one community, one people, whether we act like it or not.

The final question is not only what we believe, but whether our actions match what we say matters most.

Love and legacy are not abstract ideas we aim for in the distance. They are the sum of our decisions, repeated in our behavior day after day.

I have spent a lifetime realizing that the roots we grow are rarely planted in perfect soil. We don't get to choose the terrain, but we do get to choose how we respond to it. We grow in the ground we are given, through the choices we make, season after season.

Somewhere inside me, the boy from Jerusalem is still there. He is still observant, still resilient, and still reaching.

Still growing deeper roots.

ABOUT THE AUTHOR

Avi Shlanger arrived in the United States from Jerusalem with little money and limited English, determined to build a stable life. Through decades of dedicated work and a refusal to accept the limitations others placed on him, he built a real estate career from the ground up. Today, he is the founder and CEO of LA Apartments Biz, a company that reflects his lifelong commitment to standards, follow-through, and the belief that everyone deserves a well-managed place to call home.

Beyond the boardroom, Avi is the father of three daughters and the proud grandfather of four. He views his family as his most significant and enduring project—one that continues to grow and evolve with each passing season.

As his focus has shifted from external expansion to internal depth, Avi established the Shlanger Foundation. The initiative is dedicated to helping both teenagers and adults develop the structural integrity and resilience needed to navigate their own lives.

Roots We Grow is a candid look back at a life defined by motion, a tribute to the challenges that shaped his character, and a guide for anyone looking to grow deep enough to sustain the life they are building.

www.ingramcontent.com/pod-product-compliance
Lightning Source LLC
LaVergne TN
LVHW091150080826
845145LV00008B/2317

* 9 7 8 1 7 3 2 0 1 8 6 2 4 *